W9-APE-750

Allyn and Bacon

*Research Navigator Guide*

# The Helping Professions

Joanne Yaffe Kjosness
*University of Utah*

Linda R. Barr
*University of the Virgin Islands*

Sam Rettman

PEARSON

Boston | New York | San Francisco
Mexico City | Montreal | Toronto | London | Madrid | Munich | Paris
Hong Kong | Singapore | Tokyo | Cape Town | Sydney

For related titles and support materials, visit our online catalog at www.ablongman.com

ISBN    0-205-40832-X

Printed in the United States of America

10 9 8 7 6 5 4 3 2        08 07 06 05 04 03

# Contents

# Introduction

Your professor assigns a research paper or group report that's due in two weeks—and you need to make sure you have up-to-date, credible information. Where do you begin? Today, the easiest answer is the Internet—because it can be so convenient and there is so much information out there. But therein lies part of the problem. How do you know if the information is reliable and from a trustworthy source?

*Research Navigator Guide: The Helping Professions* is designed to help you select and evaluate research from the Web to help you find the best and most credible information you can. Throughout this guide, you'll find:

- **A Quick Guide to Research Navigator.** All you need to know to get started with Research Navigator™, a research database that gives you immediate access to hundreds of scholarly journals and other popular publications, such as *Scientific American, U.S. News & World Report,* and many others.
- **A practical and to-the-point discussion of search engines.** Find out which search engines are likely to get you the information you want and how to phrase your searches for the most effective results.
- **Detailed information on evaluating online sources.** Locate credible information on the Web and get tips for thinking critically about Web sites.
- **Citation guidelines for Web resources.** Learn the proper citation guidelines for Web sites, email messages, listservs, and more.
- **Web activities for the Helping Professions.** Explore the various ways you can use the Web in your courses through these online exercises.
- **Web links for the Helping Professions.** Begin your Web research with the discipline-specific sources listed in this section. Also included is information about Web resources offered by Allyn & Bacon—these sites are designed to give you an extra boost in your courses.

So before running straight to your browser, take the time to read through this copy of *Research Navigator Guide: The Helping Professions* and use it as a reference for all of your Web research needs.

Research Navigator™

## What Is Research Navigator™?

Research Navigator™ is the easiest way for you to start a research assignment or research paper. Complete with extensive help on the research process and three exclusive databases of credible and reliable source material (including EBSCO's ContentSelect™ Academic Journal and Abstract Database, *New York Times* Search by Subject Archive, and Link Library), Research Navigator™ helps you quickly and efficiently make the most of your research time.

**Research Navigator™ includes three databases of dependable source material to get your research process started:**

1. EBSCO's ContentSelect™ Academic Journal and Abstract Database, organized by subject, contains 50–100 of the leading academic journals per discipline. Instructors and students can search the online journals by keyword, topic, or multiple topics. Articles include abstract and citation information and can be cut, pasted, emailed, or saved for later use.

2. The *New York Times* Search by Subject Archive is organized by academic subject and searchable by keyword, or multiple keywords. Instructors and students can view full-text articles from the world's leading journalists from *The New York Times*. The *New York Times*

Search by Subject Archive is available exclusively to instructors and students through Research Navigator™.

3. Link Library, organized by subject, offers editorially selected "Best of the Web" sites. Link libraries are continually scanned and kept up to date, providing the most relevant and accurate links for research assignments.

In addition, Research Navigator™ includes extensive online content detailing the steps in the research process including:

- Starting the Research Process
- Finding and Evaluating Sources
- Citing Sources
- Internet Research
- Using your Library
- Starting to Write

# Registering with Research Navigator™

`http://www.researchnavigator.com`

Research Navigator™ is simple to use and easy to navigate. The goal of Research Navigator™ is to help you complete research assignments or research papers quickly and efficiently. The site is organized around the following tabs:

- Home
- Research Process
- Finding Sources
- Using Your Library

**In order to begin using Research Navigator™, you must first register using the personal access code that appears in the front cover of this book.**

### To Register:
4. Go to **http://www.researchnavigator.com**
5. Click "Register" under "New Users" on the left side of the screen.
6. Enter the access code exactly as it appears on the inside front cover of this book. (Note: Access codes can only be used once to complete one registration. If you purchased a used guide, the access code may not work. Please go to **www.researchnavigator.com** for information on how to obtain a new access code.)
7. Follow the instructions on screen to complete your registration—you may click the Help button at any time if you are unsure how to respond.
8. Once you have successfully completed registration, write down the Login Name and Password you just created and keep it in a safe place.

You will need to enter it each time you want to revisit Research Navigator™.

9. Once you register, you have access to all the resources in Research Navigator™ for twelve months.

## Getting Started

From the Research Navigator™ homepage, you have easy access to all of the site's main features, including a quick route to the three exclusive databases of source content that will be discussed in greater detail on the following pages. If you are new to the research process, you may want to start by clicking the *Research Process* tab, located in the upper right hand section of the page. Here you will find extensive help on all aspects of the research process, including:

- Introduction to the Research Paper
- Gathering Data
- Searching the Internet
- Evaluating Sources
- Organizing Ideas
- Writing Notes
- Drafting the Paper
- Academic Citation Styles (MLA, APA, CME, and more)
- Blending Reference Material into Your Writing
- Practicing Academic Integrity
- Revising
- Proofreading
- Editing the Final Draft

For those of you who are already familiar with the research process, you already know that the first step in completing a research assignment or research paper is to select a topic. (In some cases, your instructor may assign you a topic.) According to James D. Lester in *Writing Research Papers,* choosing a topic for the research paper can be easy (any topic will serve) yet very complicated (an informed choice is critical). He suggests selecting a person, a person's work, or a specific issue to study—President George W. Bush, John Steinbeck's *Of Mice and Men,* or learned dexterity with Nintendo games. Try to select a topic that will meet three demands.

1. It must examine a significant issue.
2. It must address a knowledgeable reader and carry that reader to another level of knowledge.
3. It must have a serious purpose, one that demands analysis of the issues, argues from a position, and explains complex details.

You can find more tips from Lester in the *Research Process* section of Research Navigator™.

Research Navigator™ simplifies your research efforts by giving you a convenient launching pad for gathering data on your topic. The site has aggregated three distinct types of source material commonly used in research assignments: academic journals (ContentSelect™); newspaper articles (*New York Times*) and world wide Web sites (Link Library).

# EBSCO's ContentSelect Academic Journal and Abstract Database

EBSCO's ContentSelect Academic Journal and Abstract Database contains scholarly, peer-reviewed journals (like the *Journal of Clinical Psychology* or the *Journal of Anthropology*). A scholarly journal is an edited collection of articles written by various authors and is published several times per year. All the issues published in one calendar year comprise a volume of that journal. For example, the *American Sociological Review* published volume 65 in the year 2000. This official journal of the American Sociological Association is published six times a year, so issues 1–6 in volume 65 are the individual issues for that year. Each issue contains between 4 and 8 articles written by a variety of authors. Additionally, journal issues may contain letters from the editor, book reviews, and comments from authors. Each issue of a journal does not necessarily revolve around a common theme. In fact, most issues contain articles on many different topics.

Scholarly journals, are similar to magazines in that they are published several times per year and contain a variety of articles in each issue, however, they are NOT magazines. What sets them apart from popular magazines like *Newsweek* or *Science News* is that the content of each issue is peer-reviewed. This means that each journal has, in addition to an editor and editorial staff, a pool of reviewers. Rather than a staff of writers who write something on assignment, journals accept submissions from academic researchers all over the world. The editor relies on these peer reviewers both to evaluate the articles, which are submitted, and to decide if they should be accepted for publication. These published articles provide you with a specialized knowledge and information about your research topic. Academic journal articles adhere to strict scientific guidelines for methodology and theoretical grounding. The information obtained in these individual articles is more scientific than information you would find in a popular magazine, newspaper article, or on a Web page.

## Using ContentSelect

Searching for articles in ContentSelect is easy! Here are some instructions and search tips to help you find articles for your research paper.

Step 1: **Select an academic subject and topic area.** When you first enter the ContentSelect Research Database, you will see a list of disciplines. To search within a single academic subject, click the name of that subject. In order to search in more than one academic subject, hold down the alt or command key. In the space below where all the subjects are listed, you must enter a topic area. For example if you choose Psychology as an academic subject you might enter "Freud" as a topic area.

Step 2: Click the **GO** button to start your search.

Step 3: **Basic Search.** By clicking **GO** you will be brought to the *Basic Search* tab. Basic Search lets you search for articles using a variety of methods. You can select from: Standard Search, All Words, Any Words, or Exact Phrase. For more information on these options, click the **Search Tips** link at any time!

Step 4: After you have selected your method Click **Search.**

**Some ways to improve your search:**

Tip 1: **Using AND, OR, and NOT** to help you search. In Standard Search, you can use AND, OR and NOT to create a very broad or very narrow search:

- **AND** searches for articles containing all of the words. For example, typing **education AND technology** will search for articles that contain **both** education AND technology.
- **OR** searches for articles that contains at least one of the terms. For example, searching for **education OR technology** will find articles that contain either education OR technology.
- **NOT** excludes words so that the articles will not include the word that follows "NOT." For example, searching for **education NOT technology** will find articles that contain the term education but NOT the term technology.

Tip 2: **Using All Words.** When you select the "All Words" option, you do not need to use the word AND—you will automatically search for articles that only contain all of the words. The order of the search words entered in does not matter. For example, typing **education technology** will search for articles that contain **both** education AND technology.

Tip 3: **Using Any Words.** After selecting the "Any Words" option, type words, a phrase, or a sentence in the window. ContentSelect will search for articles that contain any of the terms you typed (but will not search for words such as **in** and **the**). For example, type **rising medical costs in the United States** to find articles that contain *rising, medical, costs, United,* or *States.* To limit your search to find articles that contain exact terms, use *quotation marks*—for example, typing "United States" will only search for articles containing "United States."

Tip 4: **Using Exact Phrase.** Select this option to find articles containing an exact phrase. ContentSelect will search for articles that include all the words you entered, exactly as you entered them. For example, type **rising medical costs in the United States** to find articles that contain the exact phrase "rising medical costs in the United States."

### Search by Article Number

Each and every article in EBSCO's ContentSelect Academic Journal and Abstract Database is assigned its own unique article number. In some instances, you may know the exact article number for the journal article you want to retrieve. Perhaps you noted it during a prior research session on Research Navigator™. Such article numbers might also be found on the companion web site for your text, or in the text itself.

To retrieve a specific article, simply type that article number in the "Search by Article Number" field and click the **GO** button.

### Advanced Search

The following tips will help you with an Advanced Search.

Step 1: To switch to an **Advanced Search**, from the Basic Search click the *AdvancedSearch* tab on the navigation bar, just under the EBSCO Host logo. The *AdvancedSearch* tab helps you focus your search using keyword searching, search history and limiters.

Step 2: Type the words you want to search for in the **Find** field.

Step 3: Click on **Field Codes** to see a list of available field codes for limiting your search. For example: AU-Author, will limit your search to an author. Enter one of these two-letter field codes before your search term. For example, if you enter AU-Smith, this will limit your results to SMITH in the Author field. For more information on field codes, click **Search Tips**.

Step 4: After you have added the appropriate Field Code to your topic, click **Search.**

**Some ways to improve your search:**

Tip 1: You can enter additional search terms in the **Find** field, and remember to use *and, or,* and *not* to connect multiple search terms (see Tip 1 under Basic Search for information on *and, or, and not*).

Tip 2: With Advanced Searches you can also use **Limiters** and **Expanders** to refine your search. For more information on Limiters and Expanders, click **Search Tips**.

# The *New York Times* Search by Subject Archive

Newspapers, also known as periodicals because they are issued in periodic installments (e.g. daily, weekly, or monthly), provide contemporary information. Information in periodicals—journals, magazines, and newspapers—may be useful, or even critical, when you are ready to focus in on specific aspects of your topic, or to find more up-to-date information.

There are some significant differences between newspaper articles and journal articles, and you should consider the level of scholarship that is most appropriate for your research. Popular or controversial topics may not be well covered in journals, even though coverage in newspapers and "general interest" magazines like *Newsweek* and *Science* for that same topic may be extensive.

Research Navigator™ gives you access to a one-year, "search by subject" archive of articles from one of the world's leading newspapers—*The New York Times*. To learn more about *The New York Times*, visit them on the Web at **http://www.nytimes.com**.

Using the search-by-subject archive is easy. Simply type a word, or multiple words separated by commas, into the search box and click "go." You will see a list of articles that have appeared in the *New York Times* over the last year, sorted by most recent article first. You can further refine your search as needed. Articles can be printed or saved for later use in your research assignment. Be sure to review the citation rules for how to cite a newspaper article in endnotes or a bibliography.

# "Best of the Web" Link Library

The third database included on Research Navigator™, Link Library, is a collection of Web links, organized by academic subject and key terms. To use this database, simply select an academic subject from the dropdown list, and then find the key term for the topic you are searching. Click on the key term and see a list of five to seven editorially reviewed Web sites that offer educationally relevant and reliable content. For example, if your research topic is "Allergies," you may want to select the academic subject Biology and then click on "Allergies" for links to web sites that explore this topic. Simply click on the alphabet bar to view other key terms in Biology, and their corresponding links. The web links in Link Library are monitored and updated each week, reducing your incidence of finding "dead" links.

# Using Your Library

After you have selected your topic and gathered source material from the three databases of content on Research Navigator™, you may need to complete your research by going to your school library. Research Navigator™ does not try to replace the library, but rather helps you understand how to use library resources effectively and efficiently.

You may put off going to the library to complete research assignments or research papers because the library can seem overwhelming. Research Navigator™ provides a bridge to the library by taking you through a simple step-by-step overview of how to make the most of your library time. Written by a library scientist, the *Using Your Library* tab explains:

- Major types of libraries
- What the library has to offer
- How to choose the right library tools for a project
- The research process
- How to make the most of research time in the library

In addition, when you are ready to use the library to complete a research assignment or research paper, Research Navigator™ includes 31 discipline-specific "library guides" for you to use as a roadmap. Each guide includes an overview of the discipline's major subject databases, online journals, and key associations and newsgroups.

For more information and detailed walk-throughs, please visit
**www.ablongman.com/aboutRN**

*Research Navigator Guide: Helping Professions*

# Conducting Online Research

## Finding Sources:
## Search Engines and Subject Directories

Your professor has just given you an assignment to give a five minute speech on the topic "gun control." After a (hopefully brief) panic attack, you begin to think of what type of information you need before you can write the speech. To provide an interesting introduction, you decide to involve your class by taking a straw poll of their views for and against gun control, and to follow this up by giving some statistics on how many Americans favor (and oppose) gun control legislation and then by outlining the arguments on both sides of the issue. If you already know the correct URL for an authoritative Web site like Gallup Opinion Polls (www.gallup.com) or other sites you are in great shape! However, what do you do when you don't have a clue as to which Web site would have information on your topic? In these cases, many, many people routinely (and mistakenly) go to Yahoo! and type in a single term (e.g., guns). This approach is sure to bring first a smile to your face when the results offer you 200,874 hits on your topic, but just as quickly make you grind your teeth in frustration when you start scrolling down the hit list and find sites that range from gun dealerships, to reviews of the video "Young Guns," to aging fan sites for "Guns and Roses."

Finding information on a specific topic on the Web is a challenge. The more intricate your research need, the more difficult it is to find the one or two Web sites among the billions that feature the information you want. This section is designed to help you to avoid frustration and to focus in on the right site for your research by using search engines, subject directories, and meta-sites.

## Search Engines

Search engines (sometimes called search services) are becoming more numerous on the Web. Originally, they were designed to help users search the Web by topic. More recently, search engines have added features which enhance their usefulness, such as searching a particular part of the Web (e.g., only sites of educational institutions—dot.edu), retrieving just one site which the search engine touts as most relevant (like Ask Jeeves {www.aj.com}), or retrieving up to 10 sites which the search engine rank as most relevant (like Google {www.google.com}).

## Search Engine Defined

According to Cohen (1999):

> "A search engine service provides a searchable database of Internet files collected by a computer program called a wanderer, crawler, robot, worm, or spider. Indexing is created from the collected files, and the results are presented in a schematic order. There are no selection criteria for the collection of files.
>
> A search service therefore consists of three components: (1) a spider, a program that traverses the Web from link to link, identifying and reading pages; (2) an index, a database containing a copy of each Web page gathered by the spider; and (3) a search engine mechanism, software that enables users to query the index and then returns results in a schematic order (p. 31)."

One problem students often have in their use of search engines is that they are deceptively easy to use. Like our example "guns," no matter what is typed into the handy box at the top, links to numerous Web sites appear instantaneously, lulling students into a false sense of security. Since so much was retrieved, surely SOME of it must be useful. WRONG! Many Web sites retrieved will be very light on substantive content, which is not what you need for most academic endeavors. Finding just the right Web site has been likened to finding diamonds in the desert.

As you can see by the definition above, one reason for this is that most search engines use indexes developed by machines. Therefore they are indexing terms not concepts. The search engine cannot tell the difference between the keyword "crack" to mean a split in the sidewalk and "crack" referring to crack cocaine. To use search engines properly takes some skill, and this chapter will provide tips to help you use search engines more effectively. First, however, let's look at the different types of search engines with examples:

| TYPES OF SEARCH ENGINES | | |
| --- | --- | --- |
| TYPE | DESCRIPTION | EXAMPLES |
| 1st Generation | • Non-evaluative, do not evaluate results in terms of content or authority.<br>• Return results ranked by relevancy alone (number of times the term(s) entered appear, usually on the first paragraph or page of the site) | AltaVista (www.altavista.com/)<br>Excite (www.excite.com)<br>HotBot (www.HotBot.com)<br>Infoseek (guide.infoseek.com)<br>Ixquick Metasearch (ixquick.com)<br>Lycos (www.lycos.com) |
| 2nd Generation | • More creative in displaying results.<br>• Results are ordered by characteristics such as: concept, document type, Web site, popularity, etc. rather than relevancy. | Ask Jeeves (www.aj.com/)<br>Direct Hit (www.directhit.com/)<br>Google! (www.google.com/)<br>HotLinks (www.hotlinks.com/)<br>Simplifind (www.simpli.com/)<br>SurfWax (www.surfwax.com/)<br>Also see Meta-Search engines below.<br><br>EVALUATIVE SEARCH ENGINES<br>About.Com (www.about.com)<br>WebCrawler (www.webcrawler.com) |
| Commercial Portals | • Provide additional features such as: customized news, stock quotations, weather reports, shopping, etc.<br>• They want to be used as a "one stop" Web guide.<br>• They profit from prominent advertisements and fees charged to featured sites. | GONetwork (www.go.com/)<br>Google Web Directory<br>  (directory.google.com/)<br>LookSmart (www.looksmart.com/)<br>My Starting Point (www.stpt.com/)<br>Open Directory Project (dmoz.org/)<br>NetNow (www.inetnow.com)<br>Yahoo! (www.yahoo.com/) |
| Meta-Search Engines | Run searches on multiple search engines. | There are different types of meta-search engines. See the next 2 boxes. |

*(continued)*

| TYPES OF SEARCH ENGINES, *continued* | | |
|---|---|---|
| TYPE | DESCRIPTION | EXAMPLES |
| Meta-Search Engines *Integrated Result* | • Display results for search engines in one list. • Duplicates are removed. • Only portions of results from each engine are returned. | Beaucoup.com (www.beaucoup.com/) Highway 61 (www.highway61.com) Cyber411(www.cyber411. com/) Mamma (www.mamma.com/) MetaCrawler (www. metacrawler.com/) Visisimo (www.vivisimo.com) Northern Light (www.nlsearch.com/) SurfWax (www.surfwax.com) |
| Meta-Search Engines *Non-Integrated Results* | • Comprehensive search. • Displays results from each search engine in separate results sets. • Duplicates remain. • You must sift through all the sites. | Dogpile (www.dogpile.com) Global Federated Search   (jin.dis.vt.edu/fedsearch/) GoHip (www.gohip.com) Searchalot (www.searchalot.com) 1Blink (www.1blink.com) ProFusion (www. profusion.com/) |

### QUICK TIPS FOR MORE EFFECTIVE USE OF SEARCH ENGINES

1. Use a search engine:
   • When you have a narrow idea to search.
   • When you want to search the full text of countless Web pages
   • When you want to retrieve a large number of sites
   • When the features of the search engine (like searching particular parts of the Web) help with your search

2. Always use Boolean Operators to combine terms. Searching on a single term is a sure way to retrieve a very large number of Web pages, few, if any, of which are on target.
   • Always check search engine's HELP feature to see what symbols are used for the operators as these vary (e.g., some engines use the & or + symbol for AND).
   • Boolean Operators include:
     AND to narrow search and to make sure that **both** terms are included
       e.g:, children AND violence
     OR to broaden search and to make sure that **either** term is included
       e.g., child OR children OR juveniles
     NOT to **exclude** one term
       e.g., eclipse NOT lunar

*Research Navigator Guide: Helping Professions*

3. Use appropriate symbols to indicate important terms and to indicate phrases (Best Bet for Constructing a Search According to Cohen (1999): Use a plus sign (+) in front of terms you want to retrieve: +solar +eclipse. Place a phrase in double quotation marks: "solar eclipse" Put together: "+solar eclipse" "+South America").

4. Use word stemming (a.k.a. truncation) to find all variations of a word (check search engine HELP for symbols).
   - If you want to retrieve child, child's, or children use child* (some engines use other symbols such as !, #, or $)
   - Some engines automatically search singular and plural terms, check HELP to see if yours does.

5. Since search engines only search a portion of the Web, use several search engines or a meta-search engine to extend your reach.

6. Remember search engines are generally mindless drones that do not evaluate. Do not rely on them to find the best Web sites on your topic, use *subject directories* or meta-sites to enhance value (see below).

## Finding Those Diamonds in the Desert: Using Subject Directories and Meta-sites

Although some search engines, like WebCrawler (www.webcrawler.com) do evaluate the Web sites they index, most search engines do not make any judgment on the worth of the content. They just return a long—sometimes very long—list of sites that contained your keyword. However, *subject directories* exist that are developed by human indexers, usually librarians or subject experts, and are defined by Cohen (1999) as follows:

> "A subject directory is a service that offers a collection of links to Internet resources submitted by site creators or evaluators and organized into subject categories. Directory services use selection criteria for choosing links to include, though the selectivity varies among services (p. 27)."

World Wide Web Subject directories are useful when you want to see sites on your topic that have been reviewed, evaluated, and selected for their authority, accuracy, and value. They can be real time savers for students, since subject directories weed out the commercial, lightweight, or biased Web sites.

Metasites are similar to subject directories, but are more specific in nature, usually dealing with one scholarly field or discipline. Some examples of subject directories and meta-sites are found in the table on the next page.

Choose subject directories to ensure that you are searching the highest quality Web pages. As an added bonus, subject directories periodically check Web links to make sure that there are fewer dead ends and out-dated links.

## SMART SEARCHING—SUBJECT DIRECTORIES AND META-SITES

| TYPES—SUBJECT DIRECTORIES | EXAMPLES |
|---|---|
| General, covers many topics | Access to Internet and Subject Resources (www2.lib.udel.edu/subj/) |
| | Best Information on the Net (BIOTN) (http://library.sau.edu/bestinfo/) |
| | Federal Web Locator (www.infoctr.edu/fwl/) |
| | Galaxy (galaxy.einet.net) |
| | INFOMINE: Scholarly Internet Resource Collections (infomine.ucr.edu/) |
| | InfoSurf: Resources by Subject (www.library.ucsb.edu/subj/) |
| | Librarian's Index to the Internet (www.lii.org/) |
| | Martindale's "The Reference Desk" (www-sci.lib.uci.edu/HSG/ref.html) |
| | PINAKES: A Subject Launchpad (www.hw.ac.uk/libWWW/irn/pinakes/pinakes.html) |
| | Refdesk.com (www.refdesk.com) |
| | Search Engines and Subject Directories (College of New Jersey) (www.tcnj.edu/~library/research/internet_search.html) |
| | Scout Report Archives (www.scout.cs.wisc.edu/archives) |
| | Selected Reference Sites (www.mnsfld.edu/depts/lib/mu~ref.html) |
| | WWW Virtual Library (http://vlib.org) |
| Subject Oriented | |
| • Communication Studies | The Media and Communication Studies Site (www.aber.ac.uk/media) |
| | University of Iowa Department of Communication Studies (www.uiowa.edu/~commstud/resources) |
| • Cultural Studies | Sara Zupko's Cultural Studies Center (www.popcultures.com) |
| • Education | Educational Virtual Library (www.csu.edu.au/education/library.html) |
| | ERIC [Education ResourcesInformation Center] (ericir.sunsite.syr.edu/) |
| | Kathy Schrock's Guide for Educators (kathyschrock.net/abceval/index.htm) |
| • Journalism | Journalism Resources (bailiwick.lib.uiowa.edu/journalism/) |
| | Journalism and Media Criticism page (www.chss.montclair.edu/english/furr/media.html) |
| • Literature | Norton Web Source to American Literature (www.wwnorton.com/naal) |
| | Project Gutenberg [Over 3,000 full text titles] (www.gutenberg.net) |

| SMART SEARCHING, *continued* | |
|---|---|
| TYPES—SUBJECT DIRECTORIES | EXAMPLES |
| • Medicine & Health | PubMed [National Library of Medicine's index to Medical journals, 1966 to present] (www.ncbi.nlm.nih.gov/PubMed/) RxList: The Internet Drug Index (rxlist.com) Go Ask Alice (www.goaskalice.columbia.edu) [Health and sexuality] |
| • Technology | CNET.com (www.cnet.com) |

Another closely related group of sites are the *Virtual Library sites,* also referred to as Digital Library sites. Hopefully, your campus library has an outstanding Web site for both on-campus and off-campus access to resources. If not, there are several virtual library sites that you can use, although you should realize that some of the resources would be subscription based, and not accessible unless you are a student of that particular university or college. These are useful because, like the subject directories and meta-sites, experts have organized Web sites by topic and selected only those of highest quality.

You now know how to search for information and use search engines more effectively. In the next section, you will learn more tips for evaluating the information that you found.

| VIRTUAL LIBRARY SITES | |
|---|---|
| **PUBLIC LIBRARIES** | |
| • Internet Public Library | www.ipl.org |
| • Library of Congress | lcweb.loc.gov/homepage/lchp.html |
| • New York Public Library | www.nypl.org |
| University/College Libraries | |
| • Bucknell | jade.bucknell.edu/ |
| • Case Western | www.cwru.edu/uclibraries.html |
| • Dartmouth | www.dartmouth.edu/~library |
| • Duke | www.lib.duke.edu/ |
| • Franklin & Marshall | www.library.fandm.edu |
| • Harvard | www.harvard.edu/museums/ |
| • Penn State | www.libraries.psu.edu |
| • Princeton | infoshare1.princeton.edu |
| • Stanford | www.slac.stanford.edu/FIND/spires.html |
| • ULCA | www.library.ucla.edu |

*(continued)*

*Research Navigator Guide: Helping Professions*

**VIRTUAL LIBRARY SITES,** *continued*

PUBLIC LIBRARIES

Other
• Perseus Project [subject specific—classics, supported by grants from corporations and educational institutions]    www.perseus.tufts.edu

### BIBLIOGRAPHY FOR FURTHER READING

#### Books

Basch, Reva. (1996). Secrets of the Super Net Searchers.

Berkman, Robert I. (2000). *Find It Fast: How to Uncover Expert Information on Any Subject Online or in Print.* NY: HarperResource.

Glossbrenner, Alfred & Glossbrenner, Emily. (1999). *Search Engines for the World Wide Web,* 2nd Ed. Berkeley, CA: Peachpit Press.

Hock, Randolph, & Berinstein, Paula.. (1999). *The Extreme Searcher's Guide to Web Search Engines: A Handbook for the Serious Searcher.* Information Today, Inc.

Miller, Michael. *Complete Idiot's Guide to Yahoo!* (2000). Indianapolis, IN: Que.

Miller, Michael. *Complete Idiot's Guide to Online Search Secrets.* (2000). Indianapolis, IN: Que.

Paul, Nora, Williams, Margot, & Hane, Paula. (1999). *Great Scouts!: CyberGuides for Subject Searching on the Web.* Information Today, Inc.

Radford, Marie, Barnes, Susan, & Barr, Linda (2001). *Web Research: Selecting, Evaluating, and Citing* Boston. Allyn and Bacon.

#### Journal Articles

Cohen, Laura B. (1999, August). The Web as a research tool: Teaching strategies for instructors. *CHOICE Supplement* 3, 20–44.

Cohen, Laura B. (August 2000). Searching the Web: The Human Element Emerges. *CHOICE Supplement 37,* 17–31.

Introna, Lucas D., & Nissenbaum, Helen. (2000). Shaping the web: Why the politics of search engines matters. The Information Society, Vol. 16, No. 3, pp. 169–185.

# Evaluating Sources on the Web

Congratulations! You've found a great Web site. Now what? The Web site you found seems like the perfect Web site for your research. But, are you sure? Why is it perfect? What criteria are you using to determine whether this Web site suits your purpose?

Think about it. Where else on earth can anyone "publish" information regardless of the *accuracy, currency,* or *reliability* of the information? The

Internet has opened up a world of opportunity for posting and distributing information and ideas to virtually everyone, even those who might post misinformation for fun, or those with ulterior motives for promoting their point of view. Armed with the information provided in this guide, you can dig through the vast amount of useless information and misinformation on the World Wide Web to uncover the valuable information. Because practically anyone can post and distribute their ideas on the Web, you need to develop a new set of *critical thinking skills* that focus on the evaluation of the quality of information, rather than be influenced and manipulated by slick graphics and flashy moving java script.

Before the existence of online sources, the validity and accuracy of a source was more easily determined. For example, in order for a book to get to the publishing stage, it must go through many critiques, validation of facts, reviews, editorial changes and the like. Ownership of the information in the book is clear because the author's name is attached to it. The publisher's reputation is on the line too. If the book turns out to have incorrect information, reputations and money can be lost. In addition, books available in a university library are further reviewed by professional librarians and selected for library purchase because of their accuracy and value to students. Journal articles downloaded or printed from online subscription services, such as Infotrac, ProQuest, EbscoHost, or other fulltext databases, are put through the same scrutiny as the paper versions of the journals.

On the World Wide Web, however, Internet service providers (ISPs) simply give Web site authors a place to store information. The Web site author can post information that may not be validated or tested for accuracy. One mistake students typically make is to assume that all information on the Web is of equal value. Also, in the rush to get assignments in on time, students may not take the extra time to make sure that the information they are citing is accurate. It is easy just to cut and paste without really thinking about the content in a critical way. However, to make sure you are gathering accurate information and to get the best grade on your assignments, it is vital that you develop your critical ability to sift through the dirt to find the diamonds.

## Web Evaluation Criteria

So, here you are, at this potentially great site. Let's go though some ways you can determine if this site is one you can cite with confidence in your research. Keep in mind, ease of use of a Web site is an issue, but more important is learning how to determine the validity of data, facts, and statements for your use. The five traditional ways to verify a paper source can also be applied to your Web source: *accuracy, authority, objectivity, coverage,* and *currency.*

Evaluating Web Sites Using
Five Criteria to Judge Web Site Content

**Accuracy**—How reliable is the information?

**Authority**—Who is the author and what are his or her credentials?

**Objectivity**—Does the Web site present a balanced or biased point of view?

**Coverage**—Is the information comprehensive enough for your needs?

**Currency**—Is the Web site up to date?

Use additional criteria to judge Web site content, including

- **Publisher, documentation, relevance, scope, audience, appropriateness of format,** and **navigation**
- Judging whether the site is made up of **primary (original) or secondary (interpretive) sources**
- Determining whether the information is **relevant** to your research

### Content Evaluation

**Accuracy.**   Internet searches are not the same as searches of library databases because much of the information on the Web has not been edited, whereas information in databases has. It is your responsibility to make sure that the information you use in a school project is accurate. When you examine the content on a Web site or Web page, you can ask yourself a number of questions to determine whether the information is accurate.

1. Is the information reliable?
2. Do the facts from your other research contradict the facts you find on this Web page?
3. Do any misspellings and/or grammar mistakes indicate a hastily put together Web site that has not been checked for accuracy?
4. Is the content on the page verifiable through some other source? Can you find similar facts elsewhere (journals, books, or other online sources) to support the facts you see on this Web page?
5. Do you find links to other Web sites on a similar topic? If so, check those links to ascertain whether they back up the information you see on the Web page you are interested in using.
6. Is a bibliography of additional sources for research provided? Lack of a bibliography doesn't mean the page isn't accurate, but having one allows you further investigation points to check the information.
7. Does the site of a research document or study explain how the data was collected and the type of research method used to interpret the data?

If you've found a site with information that seems too good to be true, it may be. You need to verify information that you read on the Web by cross-checking against other sources.

**Authority.**   An important question to ask when you are evaluating a Web site is, "Who is the author of the information?" Do you know whether the author is a recognized authority in his or her field? Biographical information, references to publications, degrees, qualifications, and organizational affiliations can help to indicate an author's authority. For example, if you are researching the topic of laser surgery citing a medical doctor would be better than citing a college student who has had laser surgery.

The organization sponsoring the site can also provide clues about whether the information is fact or opinion. Examine how the information was gathered and the research method used to prepare the study or report. Other questions to ask include:

1. Who is responsible for the content of the page? Although a webmaster's name is often listed, this person is not necessarily responsible for the content.
2. Is the author recognized in the subject area? Does this person cite any other publications he or she has authored?
3. Does the author list his or her background or credentials (e.g., Ph.D. degree, title such as professor, or other honorary or social distinction)?
4. Is there a way to contact the author? Does the author provide a phone number or email address?
5. If the page is mounted by an organization, is it a known, reputable one?
6. How long has the organization been in existence?
7. Does the URL for the Web page end in the extension .edu or .org? Such extensions indicate authority compared to dotcoms (.com), which are commercial enterprises. (For example, www.cancer.com takes you to an online drugstore that has a cancer information page; www.cancer.org is the American Cancer Society Web site.)

A good idea is to ask yourself whether the author or organization presenting the information on the Web is an authority on the subject. If the answer is no, this may not be a good source of information.

**Objectivity.**   Every author has a point of view, and some views are more controversial than others. Journalists try to be objective by providing both sides of a story. Academics attempt to persuade readers by presenting a logical argument, which cites other scholars' work. You need to look for two sided arguments in news and information sites. For academic papers, you need to determine how the paper fits within its discipline and whether the author is using controversial methods for reporting a conclusion.

Authoritative authors situate their work within a larger discipline. This background helps readers evaluate the author's knowledge on a particular subject. You should ascertain whether the author's approach is controversial and whether he or she acknowledges this. More important, is the information being presented as fact or opinion? Authors who argue for their position provide readers with other sources that support their arguments. If no sources are cited, the material may be an opinion piece rather than an objective presentation of information. The following questions can help you determine objectivity:

1. Is the purpose of the site clearly stated, either by the author or the organization authoring the site?
2. Does the site give a balanced viewpoint or present only one side?
3. Is the information directed toward a specific group of viewers?
4. Does the site contain advertising?
5. Does the copyright belong to a person or an organization?
6. Do you see anything to indicate who is funding the site?

Everyone has a point of view. This is important to remember when you are using Web resources. A question to keep asking yourself is, What is the bias or point of *view* being expressed here?

**Coverage.** Coverage deals with the breadth and depth of information presented on a Web site. Stated another way, it is about how much information is presented and how detailed the information is. Looking at the site map or index can give you an idea about how much information is contained on a site. This isn't necessarily bad. Coverage is a criteria that is tied closely to *your* research requirement. For one assignment, a given Web site may be too general for your needs. For another assignment, that same site might be perfect. Some sites contain very little actual information because pages are filled with links to other sites. Coverage also relates to objectivity You should ask the following questions about coverage:

1. Does the author present both sides of the story or is a piece of the story missing?
2. Is the information comprehensive enough for your needs?
3. Does the site cover too much, too generally?
4. Do you need more specific information than the site can provide?
5. Does the site have an objective approach?

In addition to examining what is covered on a Web site, equally revealing is what is not covered. Missing information can reveal a bias in the material. Keep in mind that you are evaluating the information on a Web site for your research requirements.

**Currency.** Currency questions deal with the timeliness of information. However, currency is more important for some topics than for others. For example, currency is essential when you are looking for technology related topics and current events. In contrast, currency may not be relevant when you are doing research on Plato or Ancient Greece. In terms of Web sites, currency also pertains to whether the site is being kept up to date and links are being maintained. Sites on the Web are sometimes abandoned by their owners. When people move or change jobs, they may neglect to remove theft site from the company or university server. To test currency ask the following questions:

1. Does the site indicate when the content was created?
2. Does the site contain a last revised date? How old is the date? (In the early part of 2001, a university updated their Web site with a "last up dated" date of 1901! This obviously was a Y2K problem, but it does point out the need to be observant of such things!)
3. Does the author state how often he or she revises the information? Some sites are on a monthly update cycle (e.g., a government statistics page).
4. Can you tell specifically what content was revised?
5. Is the information still useful for your topic? Even if the last update is old, the site might still be worthy of use *if* the content is still valid for your research.

## Relevancy to Your Research: Primary versus Secondary Sources

Some research assignments require the use of primary (original) sources. Materials such as raw data, diaries, letters, manuscripts, and original accounts of events can be considered primary material. In most cases, these historical documents are no longer copyrighted. The Web is a great source for this type of resource.

Information that has been analyzed and previously interpreted is considered a secondary source. Sometimes secondary sources are more appropriate than primary sources. If, for example, you are asked to analyze a topic or to find an analysis of a topic, a secondary source of an analysis would be most appropriate. Ask yourself the following questions to determine whether the Web site is relevant to your research:

1. Is it a primary or secondary source?
2. Do you need a primary source?
3. Does the assignment require you to cite different types of sources? For example, are you supposed to use at least one book, one journal article, and one Web page?

You need to think critically, both visually and verbally, when evaluating Web sites. Because Web sites are designed as multimedia hypertexts, nonlinear texts, visual elements, and navigational tools are added to the evaluation process.

**Help in Evaluating Web Sites.**   One shortcut to finding high-quality Web sites is using subject directories and meta-sites, which select the Web sites they index by similar evaluation criteria to those just described. If you want to learn more about evaluating Web sites, many colleges and universities provide sites that help you evaluate Web resources. The following list contains some excellent examples of these evaluation sites:

- Evaluating Quality on the Net—Hope Tillman, Babson College
  www.hopetillman.com/findqual.html
- Critical Web Evaluation—Kurt W. Wagner, William Paterson University of New Jersey
  euphrates.wpunj.edu/faculty/wagnerk/
- Evalation Criteria—Susan Beck, New Mexico State University
  lib.nmsu.edu/instruction/evalcrit.html
- A Student's Guide to Research with the WWW
  www.slu.edu/departments/english/research/
- Evaluating Web Pages: Questions to Ask & Strategies for Getting the Answers
  www.lib.berkeley.edu/TeachingLib/Guides/Internet/EvalQuestions.html

## Critical Evaluation Web Sites

| WEB SITE AND URL | SOURCE |
| --- | --- |
| Critical Thinking in an Online World **www.library.ucsb.edu/untangle/ jones.html** | *Paper from "Untangling the Web" 1996* |
| Educom Review: Information **www.educause.edu/pub/er/review/ reviewArticles/31231.html** | *EDUCAUSE Literacy as a Liberal Art (1996 article)* |
| Evaluating Information Found on the Internet **MiltonsWeb.mse.jhu.edu/ research/education/net.html** | *University of Utah Library* |
| Evaluating Web Sites **www.lib.purdue.edu/InternetEval** | *Purdue University Library* |
| Evaluating Web Sites **www.lehigh.edu/~inref/guides/ evaluating.web.html** | *Lehigh University* |
| ICONnect: Curriculum Connections Overview **www.ala.org/ICONN/evaluate.html** | *American Library Association's technology education initiative* |
| Kathy Schrock's ABC's of Web Site Evaluation **www.kathyschrock.net/abceval/** | *Author's Web site* |

Kids Pick the best of the Web
"Top 10: Announced"
**www.ala.org/news/topkidpicks.html**

*American Library Association
initiative underwritten by
Microsoft (1998)*

Resource Selection and Information
Evaluation
**alexia.lis.uiuc.edu/~janicke/
InfoAge.html**

*Univ of Illinois, Champaign-
Urbana (Librarian)*

Testing the Surf: Criteria for Evaluating
Internet Information Sources
**info.lib.uh.edu/pr/v8/n3/
smit8n3.html**

*University of Houston Libraries*

Evaluating Web Resources
**www2.widener.edu/
Wolfgram-Memorial-Library/
webevaluation/webeval.htm**

*Widener University Library*

UCLA College Library Instruction:
Thinking Critically about World
Wide Web Resources
**www.library.ucla.edu/libraries/
college/help/critical/**

*UCLA Library*

UG OOL: Judging Quality on the Internet
**www.open.uoguelph.ca/resources/
skills/judging.html**

*University of Guelph*

Web Evaluation Criteria
**lib.nmsu.edu/instruction/
evalcrit.html**

*New Mexico State University
Library*

Web Page Credibility Checklist
**www.park.pvt.k12.md.us/academics/
research/credcheck.htm**

*Park School of Baltimore*

Evaluating Web Sites for Educational
Uses: Bibliography and Checklist
**www.unc.edu/cit/guides/irg-49.html**

*University of North Carolina*

Evaluating Web Sites
**www.lesley.edu/library/guides/
research/evaluating_web.html**

*Lesley University*

*Tip:* Can't seem to get a URL to work? If the URL doesn't begin with www,
you may need to put the http:// in front of the URL. Usually, browsers can
handle URLs that begin with www without the need to type in the "http://"
but if you find you're having trouble, add the http://.

*Research Navigator Guide: Helping Professions*

# Documentation Guidelines for Online Sources

## Your Citation for Exemplary Research

There's another detail left for us to handle—the formal citing of electronic sources in academic papers. The very factor that makes research on the Internet exciting is the same factor that makes referencing these sources challenging: their dynamic nature. A journal article exists, either in print or on microfilm, virtually forever. A document on the Internet can come, go, and change without warning. Because the purpose of citing sources is to allow another scholar to retrace your argument, a good citation allows a reader to obtain information from your primary sources, to the extent possible. This means you need to include not only information on when a source was posted on the Internet (if available) but also when you obtained the information.

The two arbiters of form for academic and scholarly writing are the Modern Language Association (MLA) and the American Psychological Association (APA); both organizations have established styles for citing electronic publications.

### MLA Style

In the fifth edition of the *MLA Handbook for Writers of Research Papers,* the MLA recommends the following formats:

- **URLs:** URLs are enclosed in angle brackets (<>) and contain the access mode identifier, the formal name for such indicators as "http" or "ftp." If a URL must be split across two lines, break it only after a slash (/). Never introduce a hyphen at the end of the first line. The URL should include all the parts necessary to identify uniquely the file/document being cited.

  ```
  <http://www.csun.edu/~rtvfdept/home/index.html>
  ```

- **An online scholarly project or reference database:** A complete "online reference contains the title of the project or database (underlined); the name of the editor of the project or database (if given); electronic publication information, including version number (if relevant and if not part of the title), date of electronic publication or latest update, and name of any sponsoring institution or organization; date of access; and electronic address.

The Perseus Project. Ed. Gregory R. Crane. Mar. 1997.
     Department of Classics, Tufts University. 15 June
     1998 <http://www.perseus.tufts.edu/>.

If you cannot find some of the information, then include the information that is available. The MLA also recommends that you print or download electronic documents, freezing them in time for future reference.

- **A document within a scholarly project or reference database:** It is much more common to use only a portion of a scholarly project or database. To cite an essay, poem, or other short work, begin this citation with the name of the author and the title of the work (in quotation marks). Then, include all the information used when citing a complete online scholarly project or reference database, however, make sure you use the URL of the specific work and not the address of the general site.

Cuthberg, Lori. "Moonwalk: Earthlings' Finest Hour."
    Discovery Channel Online. 1999. Discovery
    Channel. 25 Nov. 1999 <http://www.discovery.com/
    indep/newsfeatures/moonwalk/challenge.html>.

- **A professional or personal site:** Include the name of the person creating the site (reversed), followed by a period, the title of the site (underlined), or, if there is no title, a description such as Home page (such a description is neither placed in quotes nor underlined). Then, specify the name of any school, organization, or other institution affiliated with the site and follow it with your date of access and the URL of the page.

Packer, Andy. Home page. 1Apr. 1998 <http://
    www.suu.edu/~students/Packer.htm>.

Some electronic references are truly unique to the online domain. These include email, newsgroup postings, MUDs (multiuser domains) or MOOs (multiuser domains, object-oriented), and IRCs (Internet Relay Chats).

**Email.**    In citing email messages, begin with the writer's name (reversed) followed by a period, then the title of the message (if any) in quotations as it appears in the subject line. Next comes a description of the message, typically "Email to," and the recipient (e.g., "the author"), and finally the date of the message.

Davis, Jeffrey. "Web Writing Resources." Email to
    Nora Davis. 3 Jan. 2000.

Sommers, Laurice. "Re: College Admissions
    Practices." Email to the author. 12 Aug. 1998.

**List Servers and Newsgroups.**    In citing these references, begin with the author's name (reversed) followed by a period. Next include the title of the document (in quotes) from the subject line, followed by the words "Online posting" (not in quotes). Follow this with the date of posting. For list servers, include the date of access, the name of the list (if known), and the online address of the list's moderator or administrator. For newsgroups, follow "Online posting" with the date of posting, the date of access, and the name of the newsgroup, prefixed with "news:" and enclosed in angle brackets.

```
Applebaum, Dale. "Educational Variables." Online
    posting. 29 Jan. 1998. Higher Education
    Discussion Group. 30 Jan. 1993
    <jlucidoj@unc.edu>.
```

```
Gostl, Jack. "Re: Mr. Levitan." Online posting.
    13 June 1997. 20 June 1997
    <news:alt.edu.bronxscience>.
```

**MUDs, MOOs, and IRCs.**    Begin with the name of the speaker(s) followed by a period. Follow with the description and date of the event, the forum in which the communication took place, the date of access, and the online address. If you accessed the MOO or MUD through telnet, your citation might appear as follows:

```
Guest. Personal interview. 13 Aug. 1998.
    <telnet://du.edu:8888>.
```

For more information on MLA documentation style for online sources, check out their Web site at http://www.mla.org/style/sources.htm.

### APA Style

The newly revised *Publication Manual of the American Psychological Association* (5th ed.) now includes guidelines for Internet resources. The manual recommends that, at a minimum, a reference of an Internet source should provide a document title or description, a date (either the date of publication or update or the date of retrieval), and an address (in Internet terms, a uniform resource locator, or URL). Whenever possible, identify the authors of a document as well. It's important to remember that, unlike the MLA, the APA does not include temporary or transient sources (e.g., letters, phone calls, etc.) in its "References" page, preferring to handle them in the text. The general suggested format is as follows:

### Online periodical:

Author, A. A., Author, B. B., & Author, C. C. (2000). Title of article. *Title of Periodical, xx*, xxxxx. Retrieved month, day, year, from source.

### Online document:

Author, A. A. (2000). *Title of work.* Retrieved month, day, year, from source.

Some more specific examples are as follows:

**FTP (File Transfer Protocol) Sites.**   To cite files available for downloading via FTP, give the author's name (if known), the publication date (if available and if different from the date accessed), the full title of the paper (capitalizing only the first word and proper nouns), the date of access, and the address of the FTP site along with the full path necessary to access the file.

Deutsch, P. (1991) Archie: An electronic directory service for the Internet. Retrieved January 25, 2000 from File Transfer Protocol: ftp:// ftp.sura.net/pub/archie/docs/whatis.archie

**WWW Sites (World Wide Web).**   To cite files available for viewing or downloading via the World Wide Web, give the author's name (if known), the year of publication (if known and if different from the date accessed), the full title of the article, and the title of the complete work (if applicable) in italics. Include any additional information (such as versions, editions, or revisions) in parentheses immediately following the title. Include the date of retrieval and full URL (the http address).

Burka, L. P. (1993). A hypertext history of multi-user dungeons. *MUDdex.* Retrieved January 13, 1997 from the World Wide Web: http://www.utopia.com/ talent/lpb/muddex/essay/

Tilton, J. (1995). Composing good HTML (Vers. 2.0.6). Retrieved December 1, 1996 from the World Wide Web: http://www.cs.cmu.edu/~tilt/cgh/

**Synchronous Communications (MOOs, MUDs, IRC, etc.).**   Give the name of the speaker(s), the complete date of the conversation being referenced in parentheses, and the title of the session (if applicable). Next, list the title of the site in italics, the protocol and address (if applicable), and any directions necessary to access the work. Last, list the date of access, followed by the retrieval information. Personal interviews do not need to be listed in the References, but do need to be included in parenthetic references in the text (see the APA *Publication Manual*).

```
Cross, J. (1996, February 27). Netoric's Tuesday
    "cafe: Why use MUDs in the writing classroom?
    MediaMoo. Retrieved March 1, 1996 from File
    Transfer Protocol: ftp://daedalus.com/
    pub/ACW/NETORIC/catalog
```

**Gopher Sites.**   List the author's name (if applicable), the year of publication, the title of the file or paper, and the title of the complete work (if applicable). Include any print publication information (if available) followed by the protocol (i.e., gopher://). List the date that the file was accessed and the path necessary to access the file.

```
Massachusetts Higher Education Coordinating Council.
    (1994). Using coordination and collaboration to
    address change. Retrieved July 16, 1999 from the
    World Wide Web: gopher://gopher.mass.edu:170/
    00gopher_root%3A%5B_hecc%5D_plan
```

**Email, Listservs, and Newsgroups.**   Do not include personal email in the list of References. Although unretrievable communication such as email is not included in APA References, somewhat more public or accessible Internet postings from newsgroups or listservs may be included. See the APA *Publication Manual* for information on in-text citations.

```
Heilke, J. (1996, May 3). Webfolios. Alliance for
    Computers and Writing Discussion List. Retrieved
    December 31, 1996 from the World Wide Web:
    http://www.ttu.edu/lists/acw-1/9605/0040.html
```

Other authors and educators have proposed similar extensions to the APA style. You can find links to these pages at:

**www.psychwww.com/resource/apacrib.htm**

Remember, "frequently-referenced" does not equate to "correct" "or even "desirable." Check with your professor to see if your course or school has a preference for an extended APA style.

*Research Navigator Guide: Helping Professions*

P A R T **3**

Web
Activities

## Web Activities for the Helping Professions

### Using Usenet Newsgroups

Until a couple of years ago, Usenet newsgroups represented one of the best ways to learn about a subject area. Because of the increase in Internet traffic over the past two years, and also because of inappropriate use of Usenet to advertise commercial and often shady enterprises, it has become somewhat less useful. Still, social work and counseling students may find Usenet to be a relatively easy way to learn information about a given subject area.

### *Exercise*

Go to the Social Work Access Network (SWAN) site at **http://www.sc.edu/swan/** and click on the **SW Topics List** link on the left side of the page. Then, under *Resources,* on the left side of the page, click on the **Newsgroups** button. Click on one of the newsgroups listed (you may need to try a few before you find one your service carries). Read some of the topics available.

- What did you learn about this topic that you didn't already know?
- Are newsgroups going to provide you with authoritative information? If not, why not?

## Searching the Web for Social Work and Counseling Information

Earlier, you read about how to use Internet indexes and search engines to find information. Now you can try out some of the strategies you learned with a topic area of choice.

### *Exercise*

Select a general topic area of professional interest to you, for example, "substance abuse." Visit the search engine tutorial at **http://stauffer. queensu.ca/inforef/instruct/search.htm** and work with the information presented there about using search engines on the Web. Try using your query with at least two of the search engines listed.

- What did you learn about this topic that you didn't already know?
- Are search engines on the Web going to help you find authoritative information? How easy was it to find what you wanted?

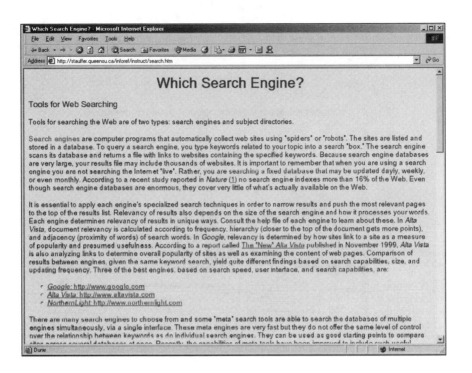

## Surfing the Web for Social Work and Counseling Information

Surfing the Web can be one of the most rewarding strategies for finding information, but you have to remain disciplined, and try not to get lost. To beat the metaphor almost to a pulp, it's easy to find yourself bobbing in the waves with the baby sea lions and the sharks if you don't keep your information objectives in mind while you are surfing.

### USING SOCIAL WORK ACADEMIC SITES

#### *Exercise*

Go to the Columbia University site at **http://www.cc.columbia.edu/ cu/ssw/.** Point your mouse cursor over **Students** on the left, and then over **Library** on the drop-down list. Click on the <u>Online Social Work Journals</u> link, and then examine the list of journals with full-text articles. Imagine being able to do some of your suggested reading without leaving the comfort of your computer! Now, select one of the listed journals to read.

- What happened when you tried to read from this journal? Why do you think this happened? Does your library provide such a service?

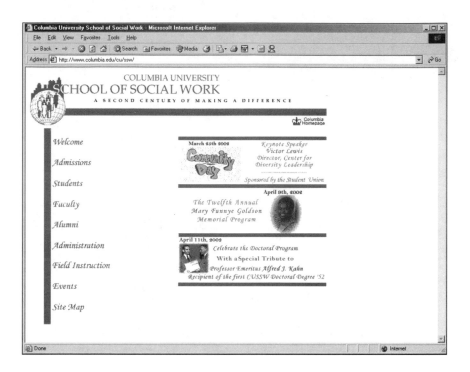

## USING GOVERNMENT RESOURCES

### Exercise

Go to the National Library of Medicine at **http://www.nlm.nih.gov/** and click on Health Information and then scroll down the page to CancerNet. Click on Cancer Literature. This will take you to the latest information the U.S. government has published on the topic of Cancer.

- How authoritative is the information presented on this site?
- How might you use information from the National Library of Medicine for your professional practice?

## USING PROFESSIONAL ASSOCIATION SITES

### Exercise

Visit the National Association of Social Workers (NASW) site at **http://www.socialworkers.org/** and click on the **Chapters** link under **ABOUT NASW** on the left of the page. Does your state chapter of NASW have email? Do they have a Web site of their own? Visit the California Chapter of NASW at **http://naswca.org.**

*Research Navigator Guide: Helping Professions*

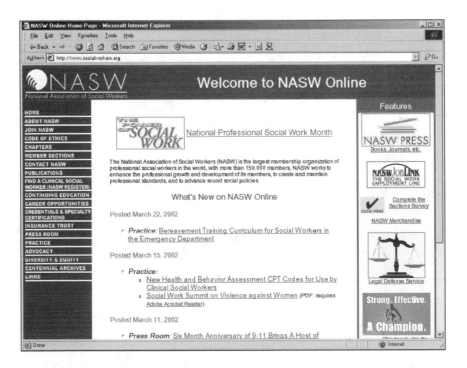

- How do you think that this site will be used by the chapter membership?
- What aspects of the site do you think will be most helpful to social workers?

## USING ELECTRONIC JOURNALS AND NEWSLETTERS

### Exercise

Go to Alcohol Alerts at **http://www.niaaa.nih.gov/publications/ alalerts.htm.** This is a quarterly bulletin of the National Institute on Alcohol Abuse and Alcoholism that disseminates important research findings on a single aspect of alcohol abuse and alcoholism. Notice that you can get free copies of these bulletins by filling out the form on the page. Select a topic of interest to you and click on the link.

- How authoritative is this information?
- How useful would this information be for writing a paper on a related topic?

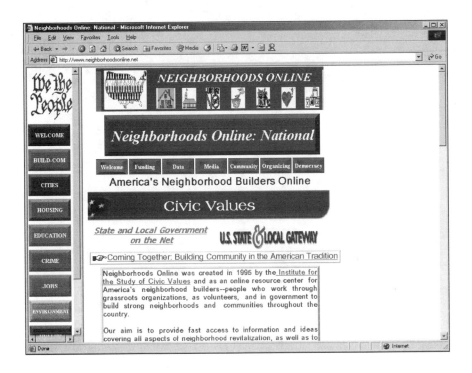

## USING SOCIAL WORK AREAS OF PRACTICE SITES

### Exercise

Go to Neighborhoods Online at **http://www.neighborhoodsonline. net/** and click on the **Community** button near the top of the page. Click on the **Neighbornets Networks** button under *Community Networking*. Now, go to **http://www.moveon.org** (Move On). We're just beginning to see the potential of the Internet as an organizing tool.

- What, if anything, was interesting about these sites? Is there anything that can be used for social work? If so, what and how?

### Exercise

Go to the Detroit Community AIDS Library at **http://www.libraries. wayne.edu/dcal/aids.html.** Click on the PubMed link under Searchable Databases. This takes you to a free Medline search page, which is a wonderful resource for finding any health-related resource.

- How useful might this resource be for you in your practice?

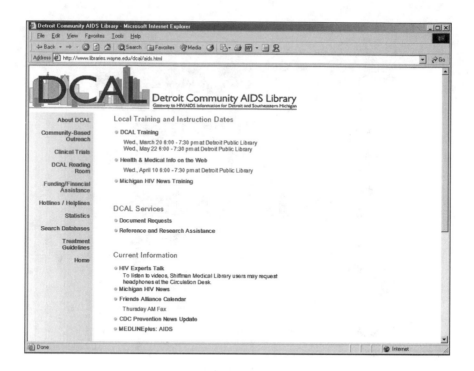

### Exercise

Go to NetPsych.com at **http://netpsych.com/**. This site explores the new uses of the Internet to deliver psychological and health care services. NetPsych is the first site to focus exclusively on online resources. Click the HUH? Button.

- What do you think of the sites you find linked here?
- What are your impressions of online psychotherapy? Should the social work profession consider an amendment to the Code of Ethics to cover practice in such circumstances?

### Exercise

Go to the Domestic Violence Handbook at **http://www.domesticviolence. org** This online resource is designed to assist women who are experiencing domestic abuse. Click on Index at the bottom of the page and follow the link to Personalized Safety Plan.

- Would you be comfortable knowing that some victims of domestic violence have no other resources to help them? Why or why not?

Online Resources

# Internet Sites Useful in Counseling

## Psychiatry

### PROFESSIONAL RESOURCES

#### Contemporary International Hypnosis

```
http://www.wiley.com/corporate/Website/Objects/
Products/0,9049,106518,00.html
```

This site is edited by G. D. Burrows, A. O., and R. Stanley, The University of Melbourne, Australia.

### PROFESSIONAL ORGANIZATIONS

#### American Psychiatric Association

```
http://www.psych.org
```

#### American Psychiatric Nurses Association

```
http://www.apna.org
```

This online resource containing legislative action alerts, government links, APNA membership, and professional resources.

### National Association of Psychiatric Health Systems

http://www.naphs.org

This behavior health care systems Web site containing membership information and resources.

### American Association of Geriatric Psychiatry

http://www.aagpgpa.org

This resource contains an AAGP bookstore, bulletins, consumer information, links to other online information, a member meeting place, and legal notices.

### Psycho Oncology

http://www.wiley.com/psychiatry/psycho.htm

The following professional references are available on this site:

- *Counseling People with Cancer,* by Mary Burton, Ph.D.
  http://www.wiley.com/psychiatry/watson.htm

- *Cancer & Emotion: A Practical Guide to Psycho-Oncology*—Third Edition, by Jennifer Barraclough.
  http://www.wiley.com/psychiatry/barra1.htm

- *Cancer and the Family—Second Edition* edited by L. Baider, C. Cooper, and A. Kaplan Denonour.
  http://www.wiley/psychiatry/baider.htm

- *Psycho Oncology Journal*
  http://www.interscience.wiley.com/jpages/1057-9249

### Psychiatric Disabilities, Employment, and the Americans with Disabilities Act Background Paper

http://www.wwws.princeton.edu/cgi-bin/
byteserv.prl/~ota/disk1/1994/9427/942701.PDF

This document evaluates current efforts under the ADA in the area of psychiatric disabilities and employment. This study was conducted by the Office of Technology Assessment.

*Research Navigator Guide: Helping Professions*

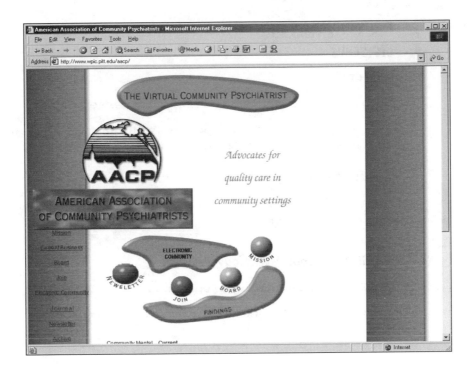

### AACP Community Psychiatrist

`http://www.communitypsychiatry.org`

A publication of the American Association of Community Psychiatrists, this site contains links with additional psychiatric resources for community mental health.

### American Association of Medical Review Office

`http://www.aamro.com`

This site contains links with educational programs, certification information, resources, and seminars.

### DSM-IV Diagnoses and Codes

`http://www.dr-bob.org/tips/dsm4a.html`

This is an alphabetical listing of diagnoses and codes. There is also a corresponding numerical listing.

## Professional Connections

### LISTSERVS

#### CataList

http://segate.sunet.se/lists/listref-eng.html

A catalogue of 26,789 public listserv lists on the Internet. Search for mailing lists of interest, and get information about listserv host sites.

#### Listserve list by Subject

http://www.mste.uiuc.edu/listserves/
subjectsearch.html

#### Global School Psychology Network

http://www.dac.neu.edu/cp/consult/

An innovative Internet Community dedicated to peer support, problem-solving assistance, professional development, and research.

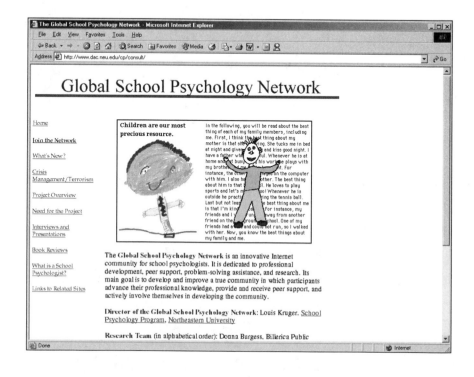

### Prevention & Treatment

`http://journals.apa.org/prevention`

Edited by Martin E. P. Seligman *Prevention & Treatment* is also free and comes with an email discussion list for subscribers to discuss the latest in psychological and psychiatric outcome/treatment research. Also included is some information on the Planetree model of patient-centered health care that is emerging as an alternative to traditional managed care.

### Counseling Today

`http://www.counseling.org/ctonline`

The Web version of *Counseling Today* has been revamped with a new look and more importantly is updated throughout the week with the latest news affecting professional counseling.

### Human Rights Education

`http://www.un.org/Pubs/CyberSchoolBus/humanrights`

The purpose of this site is to examine human rights within the context of education. Specifically, the discussion will attempt to examine the teaching of and learning about human rights within schools and the classroom.

### CESNET-L

A moderated listserv concerning counselor education and supervision, discussions about research, theory, and development of program applications pertinent to counselor education or supervision are encouraged. The listserv is concerned with the preparation and supervision of counselors in agencies, school settings, and private practice. To subscribe: subscribe CESNET-L@LISTSERV.KENT.EDU your email address.

### COUNSGRADS

COUNSGRADS has been developed to help graduate students from across the country communicate with one another. Students can talk about classes, internships, papers, and ideas about the profession. To sign up, send an email to: counsgrads@lists.acs.ohio-state.edu with the following in the body of the message: subscribe COUNSGRADS jane smith.

### Listserv Directories

`http://www.mailbase.ac.uk`
`http://www.siec.k12.in.us/~west/edu/list.htm`
`http://psychcentral.com/mail.htm`

### Government Listing

`http://www.ed.gov`

This U.S. Department of Education site includes an education kiosk, community updates, an EdInfo/listserv, Ed initiatives, Ed press releases, Ed publications published within the last ninety days, satellite town meetings, speeches, and testimonies, White House education press releases and statements, National Center for Education statistics, and school-to-work, safe and drug-free schools, Office of Vocational and Adult Education, and National Library of Education information.

### At Health, Inc.

`http://www.athealth.com`

This newsletter is distributed to over 7,300 mental health professionals.

## DISCUSSION GROUPS AND BULLETIN BOARDS

### The Network Observer

The file contains a single article from *The Network Observer,* entitled "The Art of Getting Help," which offers some guidelines about using Internet discussion groups to ask for assistance with research projects and the like. For a much longer paper that describes how to use the Net to build a professional community, send a message that looks like this:

> To: rre-request@weber.ucsd.edu
> Subject: archive send network

Network Observer is distributed through the Red Rock Eater News Service. To subscribe to RRE, send a message to the RRE server, rre-request@ weber.ucsd.edu, whose subject line reads "subscribe first name last name;" for example "Subject: subscribe Jane Doe." For more information about the Red Rock Eater, send a message to that same address with a subject line of "help." For back issues, use a subject line of "archive send index."

### School Counselors' Discussion Group

`Techsc@cblist.org`

Internet discussion group/mailing list for school counselors and counselor educators that focuses exclusively on the opportunities and implications of using emerging technology in school counseling.

### *Technology and School Counseling*

`techsc@cblist.org`

The purpose of this discussion group is to discuss methods, ideas, and resources for using technology in guidance and counseling-related activities. Group members will be encouraged to share helpful Web sites, create Internet projects with other schools, suggest Internet-based activities, express opinions and concerns about the use of technology, ask questions about purchasing software or hardware, get help with the design of their personal and/or guidance department's Web page, announce technology grants, and anything else related to the subject. This group is open to any school counselor (K–12) and counselor educator. To sign-up, go to: **http://www.cblist.org.** After entering the discussion group area, click on GUIDANCE, then click on "Techsc" (technology in school counseling) and follow the directions. To send a message to group members, simple email the message to: techsc@cblist.org

## COUNSELING DISCUSSION GROUPS

`http://www.csun.edu/~hfedp001/`
`counseling_listservs.html`

This site contains links to various discussion groups. Clicking on a link will allow you to email the group directly. Specific instructions for subscribing to some of the better groups follow.

### *CESNET-L (Counselor Education and Supervision Network)*

Counselor educators, supervisors, and students discuss research, theory, and practice related to a wide variety of professional counseling and supervision issues. To sign on, send the message: subscribe CESNET-L.

### *ACCA-L (American College Counseling Association)*

The emphasis of this list is on counseling issues with college students and the developmental and psychological issues they face while in college. College counselors and others who deal with this age group are the primary subscribers. To sign on, send the message: subscribe ACCA-L.

### *ICN (International Counselor Network)*

This network is for counselors working in all specialty areas. Topics range widely, including such issues as self-esteem, multicultural issues, program development, career planning, play theory, professional issues, and more. To sign on, send the message: subscribe ICN.

### C-PSYCH (Cross Cultural Psychology)

This is a forum for all individuals interested in cross-cultural psychology and its intertwining disciplines. To subscribe, send a message: subscribe C-PSYCH (your first name, your last name).

### PSYCGRAD (Psychology Graduate Student Project)

This list informally discusses issues of relevance to graduate students within the field of psychology and also publishes a more formal journal including student papers. To sign on, send the message: subscribe PSYCGRAD.

### EAP (Employee Assistance Counselors Net Discussion List)

EAP is a list which discusses any aspect of employee assistance counseling and psychological interventions in the workplace. To sign on, send the message: subscribe EAP.

### CARDEVNET (Career Development Network Discussion List)

CARDEVNET is a list for the discussion of issues relating to career development. To sign on, send the message: subscribe CARDEVNET.

### PSYCH-COUN

This is a discussion group for people who are interested in theoretical or research issues in counseling and psychotherapy. Students and researchers are both welcome. To sign on, send the message: subscribe PSYCH-COUNS.

### Transcultural-Psychology

This list discusses the different views of mental disorders that exist among cultures. To sign on, send the message: subscribe TRANSCULTURAL-PSYCHOLOGY.

### Survival

This list discusses topics related to domestic violence, child abuse, sexual assault and crisis/trauma intervention. The goal of the list is to provide a safe information and support network for victims of abuse and individuals who work in the field of abuse. To subscribe, send the message: subscribe SURVIVAL.

### GROUPSTUFF at Indiana University

This is a list for group workers. To subscribe, leave subject line blank, type subscribe GROUPSTUFF Internet address in the message section, then send. Note: you must use your Internet address rather than your given name in subscribing to this list. If you have difficulty, contact Rex Stockton.

### Group-Psychology

This is a list for group-therapists about processes and stages, models for group therapy, leadership and coleadership, special populations, and techniques. To subscribe, leave subject line blank, type subscribe GROUP-PSYCHOTHERAPY first name last name in the message section, then send. If you have difficulty, contact Haim Weinberg.

### NETPSY: Internet Psychology

This is a list for discussion of psychological services on the Internet. To subscribe, leave the subject line blank, type subscribe NETPSY first name last name in the message section, then send.

### PSCHYNEWS

This mental health newsletter for mental health students and professionals is accessed at: listserv@vm1.nodak.edu. To subscribe, leave the subject line blank, type subscribe PNI first name last name in the message section, then send.

### Family Therapy Networker

Family Therapy Networker Magazine has a free online mailing list where you can discuss matters related to family therapy with practitioners and Networker staff. In the subject line enter: subscribe. In the body enter: subscribe ftnetwork@intr.net.

### Psychotherapy Usenet Group

`news:sci.psychology.psychotherapy`

### School Counseling

`http://www.schoolcounselor.com`

The schoolcounselor.com Web site offers a newsletter, counseling link database, and more.

## TREATMENT SOFTWARE

### The Earley Corporation

`http://www.earleycorp.com/`

The Earley Corporation is a developer of software which assists mental health providers.

### Therascribe

`http://www.therapyshop.com/TheraScribe/`

Therascribe can produce treatment plans which are outstanding and contain all elements of JCAHO. Windows-based design.

### Therapist Helper

`http://www.quicdoc.com/Add_Ons/Therapist_Helper/`
`therapist_helper.htm`

This site contains billing and practice management software for mental health professionals. A full working demo may be downloaded.

### Therapist Traveler for the Palm Pilot

`www.helper.com/products/traveler`

This program enables providers to add new appointments to Traveler, make schedule changes, use and update contact information, and then synchronize this information with Therapist Helper at the touch of a button. With Therapist Traveler, you can have the most current and most important practice management information with you wherever you go.

### Clinical Supervision Models

`http://www.nbcc.org/`

This is the NBCC Web site for their supervision certification and model.

### The Values Realization Institute

`http://valuesrealization.org`

This nonprofit organization posts the following mission statement: The Values Realization Institute creates, supports, and empowers a network of people committed to using the Values Realization principles and concepts to positively impact the quality of life in our world community.

## PROFESSIONAL ORGANIZATIONS

### The American Psychological Association

`http://www.apa.org`

### The American Psychological Society

`http://www.psychologicalscience.org`

*Research Navigator Guide: Helping Professions*

### Association for Specialists in Group Work

http://asgw.educ.kent.edu

### American Association for Marriage and Family Therapists

http://www.aamft.org/

### American Counseling Association

http://www.counseling.org

### California Association of Marriage and Family Therapists

http://www.camft.org/

### American Association for Therapeutic Humor

http://www.aath.org/

### Association for Multicultural Counseling and Development

http://www.amcd-aaa.org

### Academy of Counseling Psychology

http://academyofabpps.org

### Association for Death Education and Counseling

http://www.adec.org/

### Association for Humanistic Psychology

http://www.ahpweb.org/

### Association for Transpersonal Psychology

http://www.atpweb.org/

### American Music Therapy Association

http://www.musictherapy.org

### American Association of Pastoral Counselors

http://www.aapc.org/

### National Coalition of Arts Therapy Associations

http://www.ncata.com/

### Sufi Psychological Association

http://www.sufi-psychology.org

## Researching Online
### BOOKSTORES

#### Amazon.com

http://www.amazon.com

This excellent online book store offers some great savings!

#### Jason Aronson, Inc

http://www.aronson.com

This site offers discounts on over 1,000 titles of works in psychotherapy, alcoholism, drug abuse, cognitive therapy, and child therapy, plus the choice of one free book for each one offered.

#### Dual Diagnosis Online Dictionary of Mental Health

http://www.human-nature.com/odmh/dual.html

Sciacca hosts this Web site for co-occurring mental illness and substance disorders. Complete articles and chapters may be read and downloaded. It also contains a search engine and mailing lists.

### ELECTRONIC JOURNALS

#### Electronic Journals and Periodicals in Psychology and Related Fields

http://www.yu.edu/ferkauf/lists/journal.htm

Here you will find an alphabetical listing of electronic journals found on the Web.

### Brown University Library of Electronic Resources

`http://www.brown.edu/Facilities/University_Library/`
`eresources/index.html`

### ERIC Articles

The latest quarterly update to the *ERIC* (Educational Resources Information Center) *Digest* database features sixty-seven full-text short reports aimed at education professionals and the broader education community. Each report includes an overview of an education topic of current interest and offers references for further information. Sample titles include *Improving Ethnic and Racial Relations in the Schools, Libraries and Democracy, Social Identity and the Adult ESL Classroom,* and *A Paradigm Shift from Instruction to Learning.* Users can search the entire ERIC Digests database from the index page. ERIC, part of the National Library of Education (NLE), is a nationwide education information system sponsored by the U.S. Department of Education's Office of Educational Research and Improvement (OERI). *ERIC Digest's* Index Page is found at: **http://www.ed.gov/ databases/ERIC_Digests/index.**

**Sample ERIC Articles.** This digest was created by ERIC, The Educational Resources Information Center. For more information about ERIC, contact ACCESS ERIC: 1-800-LET-ERIC.

**ERIC Digest.** "Helping Young Children Deal with Anger." Author: Marion, Marian. ERIC Clearinghouse on Elementary and Early Childhood Education. Champaign, IL. ED414077 97

***Helping Children Develop Self-Regulatory Skills.*** Realizing that the children in their care have a very limited ability to regulate their own emotions, teachers of infants and toddlers do a lot of self-regulation "work." As children get older, adults can gradually transfer control of the self to children so that they develop self-regulatory skills.

***Encouraging Children to Label Feelings of Anger.*** Teachers and parents can help young children produce a label for their anger by teaching them that they are having a feeling and that they can use a word to describe their angry feeling. A permanent record (a book or chart) can be made of lists of labels for anger (e.g., mad, irritated, annoyed), and the class can refer to it when discussing angry feelings.

***Encouraging Children to Talk About Anger-Arousing Interactions.*** Preschool children better understand anger and other emotions when adults explain emotions (Denham, Zoller, and Couchoud, 1994). When children

*Research Navigator Guide: Helping Professions*

are embroiled in an anger-arousing interaction, teachers can help by listening without judging, evaluating, or ordering them to feel differently.

***Using Books and Stories About Anger to Help Children Understand and Manage Anger.***    Well-presented stories about anger and other emotions validate children's feelings and give information about anger (Jalongo, 1986; Marion, 1995). It is important to preview all books about anger because some stories teach irresponsible anger management.

### SARA

This service is provided by Carfax Publishing. Contents pages for all of the journals, for those in a subject cluster, or for just one title can be requested, all free of charge! To register for this complimentary service either:

1. Access SARA (**http://www.tandf.co.uk/sara**) and follow the on-screen instructions, or
2. Send an email to SARA@carfax.co.uk with the word "info" in the body of the message.

### FIRNmail

FIRN's electronic mail (email) service features an easy to use word processing editor, online messaging, interfaces to other email systems world wide, access to limited number of Internet services, and a conferencing system which serves as a bulletin board service. The phone number for FIRN Support Staff/Help desk is (800-749-3476)

## PROFESSIONAL RESOURCES

### Guides to Internet Resources

http://www.clearinghouse.net

The Argus Clearinghouse offers a large collection of guides to Internet resources categorized by topic.

### Federal Government Information

http://www.lib.lsu.edu/gov/fedgov.html

This is the Louisiana State University Libraries United States Federal Government Agencies Page.

### Library Catalogs

http://www.libdex.com

LibDex is a directory of library catalogs which can be searched via the Web.

*Research Navigator Guide: Helping Professions*

### Library of Congress

http://www.lcweb.loc.gov/catalog

This site provides access to the holdings of the Library of Congress, United States Government copyright files, federal legislation, foreign law, and gateway access to many other library catalogs.

### Brief Counseling That Works: A Solution-Focused Approach for School Counselors

This title can be ordered directly from the publisher:

http://www.corwinpress.com

### Department Home Page Human Development and Family Science Extension

http://www.hec.ohio-state.edu/famlife/index.htm

### National Network for Family Resiliency

http://www.nnfr.org

### Counseling Center Village

http://ub-counseling.buffalo.edu/ccv.html

## 1 AND 2 CURRICULUM

### MARCO

A counselor-owned and operated company, MARCO is accessible at 1-800-448-2197. Their offerings include:

- Lions Quest Skills
- Here's Looking at You 2000
- The Name Game
- Facts About Friends
- Handling Anger
- Study Skills 1 & 2
- Classroom Guidance Activities
- Classroom Guidance Primary and Intermediate
- 102 Tools for Teachers & Counselors, Too.

### Paperbacks for Education

Bibliotherapy books arranged by topic that helps with selecting books to use in class and groups. 1-800-227-2591.

### Connecting with Others: Lessons for Teaching Social and Emotional Competence

http://www.researchpress.com/scripts/
product.asp?item=4917

Volumes are available for K–2, 3–5, 6–8, and 9–12.

### The School Counselor's Book of Lists

This book is available for examination free for thirty days by calling 1-800-288-4745. The order # is C1293–4. If you decide to purchase the book, it is $32.95 plus postage.

### Community Peacemakers

http://www.compeace.org

This site, geared toward educators, is full of counseling material for classroom use. For more information about the program's organizer, Community Peacemakers, please send an email to: compeace@concentric.net

## PROFESSIONAL SERVICES

### American Academy of Pediatrics

http://www.aap.org

This Web site is committed to the attainment of optimal physical, mental, and social health for all infants, children, adolescents, and young adults.

### The American Psychiatric Association

http://www.psych.org

The American Psychiatric Association is a national medical specialty society whose 40,500 physician members specialize in the diagnosis and treatment of mental and emotional illnesses and substance use disorders.

### American Psychological Association (APA)

http://www.apa.org/about/division/div28.html

This is the home page for the Division of Psychopharmacology and Substance Abuse of the American Psychological Association. Of interest to psychologists practicing in the drug abuse field may be the Web site for the APA College of Professional Psychology.

### American Psychological Society (APS)

http://www.psychologicalscience.org

Advancing the scientific discipline and the giving away of psychology in the public interest is the aim of this site.

### American Public Health Association

http://www.apha.org

The American Public Health Association (APHA) is the oldest and largest organization of public health professionals in the world, representing more than 50,000 members from over fifty occupations of public health. The Association and its members have been influencing policies and setting priorities in public health since 1872.

### Brian Disorders Network

http://www.brainnet.org

The Brain Disorders Network is sponsored by the National Foundation for Brain Research.

### The Centers for Disease Control and Prevention (CDC)

http://www.cdc.gov

The Centers for Disease Control and Prevention (CDC), located in Atlanta, Georgia, USA, is an agency of the Public Health Service, in the Department of Health and Human Services. Its mission is to promote health and quality of life by preventing and controlling disease, injury, and disability.

### National Alliance for Hispanic Health

http://www.hispanichealth.org

Its mission is to improve the health and well-being of all Hispanic communities throughout the United States.

### The Institute of Behavioral Research at TCU

http://www.ibr.tcu.edu

The Institute of Behavioral Research (IBR) at TCU conducts evaluations of drug abuse and addiction services. Special attention is given to assessing and analyzing individual functioning, treatment delivery, and engagement process, and their relationships to outcomes. Treatment improvement protocols developed and tested emphasize cognitive and behavioral strategies for programs in community-bases as well as criminal justice settings. Its people, projects, publications, and training programs are described, and a variety of data collection forms are available for downloading.

### National Criminal Justice Reference Service (NCJRS)

http://www.whitehousedrugpolicy.gov
http://www.ncjrs.org/

The National Criminal Justice Reference Service (NCJRS) is one of the most extensive sources of information on criminal and juvenile justice in the world, providing services to an international community of policymakers and professionals. NCJRS is a collection of clearing-houses supporting all bureaus of the U.S. Department of Justice, Office of Justice Programs: the National Institute of Justice, the Office of Juvenile Justice and Delinquency Prevention, the Bureau of Justice Statistics, the Bureau of Justice Assistance, the Office for Victims of Crime, and the OJP Program Offices. It also supports the Office of National Drug Control Policy. National Families in Action (NFIA).

### National Families in Action (NFIA)

http://www.emory.edu/NFIA

A private, nonprofit membership organization founded in 1977. It helped create and lead the parent movement, the first tier of the prevention movement that drove drug use down by two-thirds among adolescents and young adults between 1979 and 1992. Its goal is to help parents prevent drug abuse in their families and communities.

### National Library of Medicine

http://www.nlm.nih.gov

The National Library of Medicine is the world's largest library dealing with a single scientific/professional topic. It cares for over 4.5 million holdings (including books, journal, reports, manuscripts, and audio-visual items).

### National Board for Certified Counselors (NBCC)

http://www.nbcc.org/

This site contains listings for information on state and national credentialing, graduate student updates, bulletins, and a newsletter with NCC LINC. Also included is an RACC bulletin which contains information on summer fellowships.

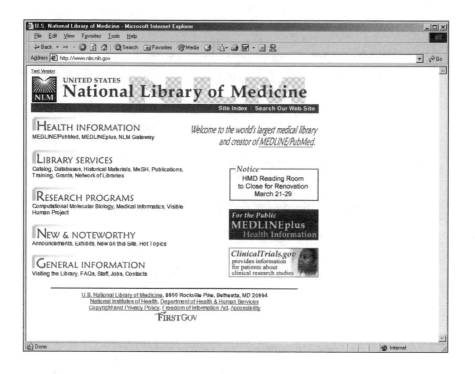

### The Internet: A Tool for Career Planning

`http://www.ncda.org/crstore/books.html#3`

Published by NCDA (National Career Development Association), *The Internet: A Tool for Career Planning,* is coauthored by Joann Harris-Bowlsbey, Margaret Riley Kikel, and James P. Sampson, Jr. Single copies are $20, $10 for NCDA members.

## Career Counseling Resources

### CAREER GUIDANCE

#### ACAeNews

`http://www.counseling.org/enews/volume_2/0202a.htm`

ACAeNews begins a two-part series on anticipated changes in career guidance and counseling in schools. Changing United States demographics demand broader perspectives of professionals who must prepare the next generation of workers. Part one addresses key historical issues, explores the role of the school counselor in career counseling, and compares career education versus career guidance.

### College is Possible

`http://www.CollegeIsPossible.org`

Created by the Coalition of America's Colleges, this site is offered as a guide for parents and students to information and advice on higher education, especially with regard to financial matters. The site is composed of three primary sections: Preparing for College, Choosing the Right College, and Paying for College. The first section offers a ten-step guide (beginning with pre-school), recommended secondary school courses, and an electronic and print resource library.

### Internet Guide for College Bound Students

`http://www.amazon.com`

Published by The College Board, the book is available online (**www. amazon.com**) or in bookstores. Chapters contain resources for college exploration.

### The Student Center

`http://www.counseling.org/enews/volume_2/0202b.htm`

Volunteering with professionals and agencies. Developing real working relationships with educators, professionals, and agencies as a volunteer can be a helpful way to gain valuable experiences and maybe get an edge in your future job hunt.

### Lynn Friedman, Ph.D.'s Web Site

`http://www.drlynnfriedman.com`

This site provides answers to questions about the trials and tribulations in the workplace, dealing with challenging interpersonal situations, negotiating salary, finding a better job, and establishing and pursuing life goals at work and in life.

### Career Journal from the Wall Street Journal

`http://www.careerjournal.com`

A most excellent resource, this is a listing of online job databases and related tools and sites.

### Careerware: Career Aptitude Survey

`http://www.careerware.com/products/us/cas.htm`

Careerware. Computerized aptitude test for 8th grade to adult known as the Career Aptitude Survey. The CAS, which is a timed/standardized/

computerized aptitude test, encompasses 5 areas: Verbal Comprehension, Numerical Ability, Visual Speed and Accuracy, Space Visualization, and Numerical Reasoning. Also available: a broad spectrum of computerized career development software available for upper elementary, middle school, high school, college, and beyond, as well as many other supplemental products necessary for building a successful career center or career program at your site.

### EXPLORE

`www.act.org/explore`

ACT's eighth grade program includes a workbook in which students develop a four year plan based on the results of the Interest Inventory, UNI-ACT, and the results of their achievement scores in English, math, reading, and science reasoning.

### Career Counseling Netserve

`Email: cardevnet-request@world.std.com`

This site lists counseling discussion groups. From there you can click on CARDEVNET (Career Development Network Discussion List). To sign on, send the message (in the body, no subject), subscribe (no quotation marks).

## VOCATIONAL EDUCATION/SCHOOL-TO-WORK

### National Center for Research in Vocational Education

`http://vocserve.berkeley.edu/SkillsPage.html`

This site includes full texts of newsletters, monographs, and other reports produced by NCRVE. It also includes skill standards links, a calendar of events, and a listing of school-to-work technical assistance providers. A mini-catalogue can be found at:

### New York Department of Labor

`http://www.labor.state.ny.us/labor_market/`
`LMI_educators/LMI_educators.html`

This site focuses on youth career and has information about choosing a career, acquiring needed skills, finding a job, and tools for educators. It also has links to working papers and a career resource library.

### Office of Vocational and Adult Education

`http://www.ed.gov/offices/OVAE`

This site includes a variety of information about initiatives, resources, grants, technical assistance providers, research, and events.

### Education Week

`http://www.edweek.org/context/topics/`
`issuepage.cfm?id=24`

The *Education Week* newspaper has a site containing school-to-work articles from its archives. It also provides other print and Web resources on school-to-work.

### Minnesota School-to-Work: School Activities

`http://children.state.mn.us/stw/school.html/`
`best/Teacher.htm`

Find out why Minnesota's School-to-Work program is so effective. Not only do students visit workplaces and perform real work there, but so do teachers, as Brian A. Bottge and Lynne S. Osterman discuss in *Bringing the Workplace to the Classroom.*

## PORTFOLIOS

### Federal Employment Opportunities

`http://www.usajobs.opm.gov`

This site contains job listing from the Veterans Administration.

### HealthCareerWeb

`http://www.healthcareerweb.com`

This site provides services for job seekers and includes a job search feature, a resume database, and a free job-match service. The site also markets products.

### America's Career InfoNet

`http://www.acinet.org`

This site offers registered users America's Job Bank listing of thousands of job vacancies and America's Talent Bank for employers in search of a database of resumes.

## CAREER DEVELOPMENT COMPUTER SOFTWARE

### *COIN*

http://www.coin3.com

This Guidance Program comes in both Windows and Mac platforms. It is a very complete program. COIN Educational Products, Inc, can be reached at 1-800-274-8515.

# School Counseling Resources

## GUIDANCE CURRICULUM

### *Classroom Guidance Activities*

http://www.educationalmedia.com/home.html-ssi

Elementary School Counselors will enjoy this Sourcebook. (There is also an edition available for Secondary School Counselors.) The authors are; Joe Wittmer, Ph.D., Diane W. Thompson, Ed.S., and Larry C. Loesch, Ph.D. If you would like to order a copy of this book you can write or call the publisher at Educational Media Corporation, PO Box 21311, Minneapolis, MN 55421-0311, (612) 781-0088. The cost of the book is $24.95.

### *I Am Responsible*

http://teacher.scholastic.com/lessonrepro/
lessonplans/theme/resp48.htm

This integrated theme unit connects classroom learning and life lessons.

### *We Are Family*

http://teacher.scholastic.com/lessonrepro/
lessonplans/theme/fam23.htm

This integrated theme unit explores all kinds of families. You can choose from Kindergarten through grade 1, grades 2 to 3, and grades 4 to 8.

### *Test Anxiety and Stress Workshops*

http://ub-counseling.buffalo.edu/ccv.html

The Counseling Center Village. A good resource for workshops, with outlines on stress management and test anxiety.

### Relaxation Training

Available on http://www.amazon.com:

- *Don't Despair on Thursdays!* The Children's Grief-Management Book (The Emotional Impact Series). Adolph Moser, et. al., School & Library Binding, 1998. Usually ships in twenty-four hours.
- *Don't Feed the Monster on Tuesdays!* The Children's Self-Esteem Book. Adolph J. Moser, et. al., School & Library Binding, 1991. Usually ships in twenty-four hours.
- *Don't Pop Your Cork on Mondays!* The Children's Anti-Stress Book. Adolph J. Moser, Dav Pilkey (Illustrator), School & Library Binding, 1988. Usually ships in twenty-four hours.
- *Don't Rant and Rave on Wednesdays!* The Children's Anger-Control Book. Adolph Moser, et. al., School & Library Binding, 1994.

### Bibliotherapy in Elementary Schools

`http://www.indiana.edu/~eric_rec/ieo/`
`bibs/bibl-ele.html`

This is a useful site for conducting bibliocounseling with elementary students.

### Susquehanna Institute

`http://www.susquehanna-institute.com`

Help support free and low-cost counseling by ordering books, CDs, videos, and games.

### New One-Stop for Department Publications

`http://www.ed.gov/about/ordering.jsp`

Ed Pubs is the Department of Education's one-stop shop for information products. Ed Pubs (short for Education Publications Center) is the place to call for publications, brochures, videos, CD-ROMs, posters, bookmarks, and other Ed products. Ed Pubs include online ordering via the Internet, a searchable database that includes all Ed products, a customer call center, and an automated inventory system for Ed personnel. Ed Pubs customer service representatives (including Spanish speaking representatives) are available from 9 A.M. to 6 P.M. (ET), Monday through Friday. You may call any time to leave a voicemail request or to use the fax-on-demand service.

### Education World

`http://db.education-world.com/perl/browse?cat_id=589`

## ERIC/CASS (Under ERIC)

`http://ericcass.uncg.edu`

Clearinghouse (ERIC/CASS). The original clearinghouse was established in 1966 by Dr. Garry R. Walz at the University of Michigan and has been in continuous operation since that date. Its scope area includes school counseling, school social work, school psychology, mental health counseling, marriage and family counseling, career counseling, and student development, as well as parent, student, and teacher education in the human resources area. Topics covered by ERIC/CASS include training, supervision, and continuing professional development; human services and mental health professionals; counseling theories, methods, and practices; the roles of counselors, social workers, and psychologists in all the education settings at all levels; career planning and development; self-esteem and self-efficacy; marriage and family counseling; and counseling services to special populations such as substance abusers, pregnant teenagers, students at risk, and public offenders.

Fifty Research Syntheses have been added recently to a full-text searchable database of 2,000 such syntheses on the Department's Web site at: **http://www.ed.gov/databases/ERIC_Digests/index.**

The following are the titles of the 50 ERIC Digests:

| FILE NAME | FILE TITLE |
| --- | --- |
| ed419326 | Rights & Responsibilities of Parents of Children with Disabilities. |
| ed419385 | Secondary Newcomer Programs: Helping Recent Immigrants Prepare for School Success. |
| ed419624 | Loneliness in Young Children. |
| ed419625 | Failure Syndrome Students. |
| ed419632 | Father Involvement in Schools. |
| ed420302 | The Benefits of Information Technology. |
| ed420303 | Internet Resources for K–8 Students. |
| ed420305 | An Introduction to Internet Resources for K–12 Educators. Part I: Information Resources, Update 1998. |
| ed420306 | An Introduction to Internet Resources for K–12 Educators. Part II: Question Answering, Listservs, Discussion Groups, Update 1998. |
| ed420897 | Creating a Learning Organization. |
| ed421179 | Forces Motivating Institutional Reform. |
| ed421180 | Using Technology in Remedial Education. |
| ed421181 | Responding to Accountability Mandates. |
| ed421281 | Motivation and Middle School Students. |
| ed421447 | A Global Perspective on Human Rights Education. |
| ed421480 | Promoting Stress Management: The Role of Comprehensive School Health Programs. |
| ed421481 | Service-Learning and Teacher Education. |
| ed421483 | True and Quasi-Experimental Designs. |
| ed421484 | Statewide Assessment Programs: Policies and Practices for the Inclusion of Limited English Proficient Students. |
| ed421485 | Designing Structured Interviews for Educational Research. |
| ed421486 | Herzberg's Theory of Motivation and Maslow's Hierarchy of Needs. |
| ed416940 | Effective Policies for Remedial Education. |
| ed416941 | Faculty and Staff Development. |
| ed417123 | Trends in Peace Education. |
| ed417124 | Global Education: Internet Resources. |
| ed417244 | Improving School Violence Prevention Programs through Meaningful Evaluation. |
| ed417501 | Reducing the Disproportionate Representation of Minority Students in Special Education. |
| ed417515 | School-Wide Behavioral Management Systems. |
| ed418249 | New Perspectives on Mentoring. |

| | |
|---|---|
| ed418654 | Faculty Workload Studies: Perspectives, Needs, and Future Directions. |
| ed418832 | Building School-to-Work Systems in Rural America. |
| ed419029 | Recent Changes in School Desegregation. |
| ed419030 | The Challenges of Parent Involvement Research. |
| ed419031 | Parent Engagement as a School Reform Strategy. |

### Access Eric

`http://www.eric.ed.gov`

This is the gateway to the Internet sites of the Educational Resources Information Center (ERIC).

### AskEric/Lesson Plans

`http://ericir.syr.edu/Virtual/Lessons`

The AskERIC Virtual Library contains hundreds of lesson plans, including, but not limited to, language arts, mathematics, social studies, and science. Also included are lesson plans from School Library Media Activities Monthly, Newton's Apple Educators Guides, and Crossroads: K16 American History Curriculum.

### Benard's Urban Ed

`http://eric-web.tc.columbia.edu/digests/dig126.html`

This site is a clearinghouse ERIC Digest, Turning it around for all youth: from risk to resilience.

### Acceptable Use Policies

`http://chico.rice.edu/armadillo/Rice/Resources/`
`acceptable.html`

Many schools which provide Internet access to students and staff have created policies and agreements for the appropriate use of Internet accounts. Samples of agreements, policies, and opinion pieces have been collected at Armadillo's World Wide Web server.

### A Tour of the World Wide Web for School Counselors

`http://www.thejournal.com/magazine/vault/A1914.cfm`

*Research Navigator Guide: Helping Professions*

### World School Directory

`http://www.education-world.com/regional/k12_schools`

This site is a country-by-country and state-by-state guide to K12 Schools, Universities, and Education Resources around the world. Users can find the following LOCAL Schools within this guide:

- Charter Schools & School Districts
- Montessori Schools
- Parochial Schools & School Districts
- Private Schools
- Public Schools & School Districts
- Gifted and Talented School Districts
- Special Needs School Districts
- Universities & University Departments

Also available are the following related resources:

- Education Organizations
- K12 School Libraries
- School Newspapers
- K12 School Publications
- Alumni Publications
- Regional Education Resources
- Vocational—Technical Schools
- Gifted and Talented School
- International School
- Magnet Schools
- Online Schools
- Special Needs Schools

### Goals 2000

`http://www.ed.gov/pubs/G2KReforming`

*Goals 2000: Reforming Education to Improve Student Achievement* (April 1998) looks at how Goals 2000 supports state efforts to develop clear and rigorous standards for what every child should know and be able to do, and supports comprehensive state- and district-wide planning and implementation of school efforts focused on improving student achievement of those standards.

### ASCD Education Bulletin

`Email: Bulletin@listserv.ascd.org`

This biweekly online newsletter of the Association for Supervision and Curriculum Development (ASCD) International is dedicated to sharing and exchanging information on the issues of international development, democracy, and professional development.

### American School Counselors Association Materials

`http://www.schoolcounselor.org`

ASCA has also developed national standards for school counselors. Descriptions of the duties and goals of school counselors are listed. Copies are available on their Web site along with *Get a Life Portfolio* (in single or bulk rates):

- *Facilitator's Manual*—eight chapters of practical information and in-service activities for local staff and community helpers (131 pages).
- *Facilitator's Guide*—5-page quick-reference guide to help teachers and advisors maximize the *Get A Life Portfolio.*
- *Introductory Video* (10 minutes)—introduces the program to school staff, parents, and community groups.
- *Get A Life Software*—storage, retrieval, and editing software to help track student goals (DOS compatible, 3-½" disks).
- *Macintosh Programming Guide*—for customizing the program and creating word processing files on a Macintosh computer.

### Counselor Connection

`http://ericass.uncg.edu/CounselorConnection.html`

This site has links to numerous articles and resources for school counselors. Issues covered relate to bullying, substance abuse, violence, suicide, gangs, career development, student achievement, cultural diversity, conflict resolution, and the list goes on and on.

### Transitioning

`http://www.middleweb.com/INCASE5to6.html`

A collection of good ideas for fifth–sixth grade transitioning.

### Books for Middle School

All of the following are available from **www. amazon.com**

- *Enjoy Your Middle Schooler: A Guide to Understanding the Physical, Social, Emotional, and Spiritual Changes of Your eleven- to fourteen-Year-Old,* by Wayne Rice.
- *Middle School Blues,* by Lou Kassem.
- *The Middle School Maze*, by Cliff Schimmels.
- *The Parents' Public School Handbook: How to Make the Most of Your Child's Education, from Kindergarten Through Middle School,* by Kenneth Shore.

### ACPS Middle Schools 24

http://www.acps.k12.va.us/sitemap.html

This Web site displays a suggested time line for preschool to early elementary school transition.

### Transition and Continuity between Head Start and Public Schools

http://www.psy.miami.edu/faculty/dgreenfield/research

This site includes benefits of transition, keys to successful transition key concepts about transition to kindergarten, a transition checklist, differences between early childhood and kindergarten, and a kindergarten observer's worksheet.

### Behavioral Interventions

Email: vstanhope@naspweb.org

The newly released publication from the Center, *Behavioral Interventions: Creating a Safe Environment in Our Schools* discusses behavioral problems in children, highlighting positive strategies and interventions. To request a free copy of *Behavioral Interventions,* email Victoria Stanhope at vstanhope@naspweb.org and give your regular mailing address.

### Communities That Care

http://www.cisnet.org
http://www.americaspromise.org

For information on how to become one of Colin Powell's Schools of Promise, visit this Web site or that of Communities in Schools.

### Learning Style Inventory

http://www.howtolearn.com/personal.html

Twenty-four item learning style online survey. An evaluation tool to assess learning styles. Identifies visual/auditory/tactile learners and gives a description of each style.

### K–12 Practitioners Home Page—NCES

http://nces.ed.gov/practitioners

The National Center for Education Statistics (NCES) has launched a site for K–12 practitioners that summarizes and explains some of the latest educational research findings. Survey data that support these findings, as well as methods used to conduct the surveys are outlined. Teachers, administrators, school support staff, and parents can examine articles in the Research Findings section on topics such as Teacher Job Satisfaction, At-Risk Students, and the Pipeline to Higher Education. Links to additional NCES resources and organizations affiliated with NCES projects are also included.

### Idea Book

`http://www.ed.gov/pubs/Idea_Planning`

*Implementing Schoolwide Programs: An Idea Book on Planning* presents methods and resources for planning schoolwide programs and for measuring their success. It also focuses on the fact that schoolwide programs have the flexibility to combine many federal education funds with state and local funds to operate. Featured are schools that have a record of improving student performance; cohesive planning; a comprehensive, standards-based curriculum; highly qualified staff who are committed to building a culture of learning; family, school, and community partnerships that have helped sustain the school's academic achievements and have combined Title I funds with state and local resources.

### Simulation Games

`http://www.stsintl.com/schools/bafa.html`

BaFa BaFa (racism and culture) is a simulation game that aims to let groups experience racist feelings toward each other, based on two hypothetical "cultures." In debriefing they will realize how racism can be based on misinformation and wrong perceptions, as well as understand how interaction can help overcome racial barriers. This can also be adapted to highlight communication between any two groups, such as parents–teens, different language groups, and different schools.

### Education World®

`http://www.education-world.com`
`http://www.education-world.com/a_curr/curr125.shtml`

This site where educators go to learn is a database of over 110,000 sites featuring what's new, education topics, guide site reviews, world resource center, world school directory, cool schools, employment listings, events calendar, distribution lists, message boards, questionnaire, and awards and accolades.

### 7 Habits

```
http://www.usaweekend.com/99_issues/990124/
990124coveyhour.html
```

Let the *7 Habits* author and *USA Weekend* contributing editor show you how to better realize life goals with quizzes and articles at the Stephen Covey Archive.

### School Psychology Resource Online

```
http://www.schoolpsychology.net
```

This is an online resource for the school psychology community. Information on learning disabilities, ADHD, gifted, autism, adolescence, parenting, and assessment are just a few of the many resources offered.

### Global School Psychologist Network

```
http://www.dac.neu.edu/cp/consult/
```

This site is moderated by Dr. L. Kruger.

## Study Guides

http://www.iss.stthomas.edu/studyguides

*Study Guides* includes over fifty pages of summary guides to assist students in succeeding in their studies. Topics include time and stress management, test preparation, organizational strategies, reading and writing, and more. Translated into Arabic, Russian, Chinese, French, German, and Italian, the site should help students around the world. Grade level: high school. College content area: education (teaching and learning). Application type: resource.

## Consortium for School Networking (CoSN)

http://www.cosn.org

## Certified Cognitive-Behavioral School Counselor

http://www.nacbt.org

For a grandfathering application, call 1-800-853-1135 or email with your name and street address to nacbt@nacbt.org.

## Icebreakers and Energizers

http://www.kimskorner4teachertalk.com/
classmanagement/icebreakers.html

This site includes some of the traditional ideas such as "people bingo" but has others as well.

## Teaching Young Children How to Visualize

ASCD Education Bulletin

The biweekly online newsletter of the Association for Supervision and Curriculum Development. To subscribe:

Email:
To: BULLETIN@LISTSERV.ASCD.ORG
Subject: ASCD Education Bulletin

## Nicenet

http://www.nicenet.org

Nicenet is a way for educators to set up a Web page without having to format anything. Type in the information. Try setting up a temporary account so you can view its features.

### Teacher/Advisor Site

http://www.mentors.ca

This site includes an annotated bibliography that is searchable and contains virtually every published article about the Teacher–Advisor system. Seminars are provided on establishing such systems, and the Web site includes details about that curriculum as well.

### Peer Counseling/Mentoring/Helping Sites

http://www.islandnet.com/~rcarr
http://www.peerhelping.org

### Research Papers

http://www.peer.ca/Docs.html.

Read one of the papers available online or access all the published literature about peer mediation.

### School Psychology Resources Online

http://www.schoolpsychology.net

### Student Counseling Centers on the Internet

http://ub-counseling.buffalo.edu

### WCN (Interactive Counseling Community)

http://www.CounselingNetwork.com

### Sexual Harrassment Site

http://www.schoolcounselor.com/harass.htm

### Confronting Sexual Harassment: Learning Activities for Teens

http://www.educationalmedia.com/bookfiles/
confsexualharas.html

Help your teenagers develop positive personal relationships and confront the troublesome area of sexual harassment. Eight group sessions and twenty-seven supplementary activities are provided to challenge students from ages twelve to eighteen to take more responsibility in creating a safe and productive school environment. Included are reproducible activity sheets and assessment instruments. Use with individuals, small groups, classrooms, or community groups by Russell A. Sabella and Robert D. Myrick, Ph.D.

## COUNSELING SPECIAL CLIENT POPULATIONS

### Annotated Guide to a Parent's Research for Gifted Children

http://www.stephanietolan.com/is_it_a_cheetah.htm

*Is It A Cheetah?* by Stephanie Tolan. This essay uses the analogy of identifying, classifying, and caging a cheetah to address some of the problems associated with raising, teaching, or being a gifted child. Good light reading.

http://www.nexus.edu.au/teachstud/gat/evanss.htm

*Acceleration: A Legitimate Means of Meeting the Needs of Gifted Children,* by Dr. Sarah Evans. The "best of the bunch," this critical review of accelerative methods and motivations thoroughly examines arguments both for and against acceleration in all its forms.

http://www.gifteddevelopment.com/
Whatwe'velearned.html

*What We Have Learned About Gifted Children,* by Linda Silverman. Key findings indicate that gifted children need different teaching methods from non-gifted learners, and that gifted children have better social adjustment in classes with children like themselves, whether age-peer gifted or intellectual peers.

http://www.edweek.org/ew/vol-16/07winner.h16

*The Miseducation of Our Gifted Children,* by Ellen Winner, in *Education Week.* Providing special education to gifted children offends our egalitarian sensibilities, but we need to recognize the importance of appropriate education techniques to teaching gifted children.

http://www.hoagiesgifted.org/struggle.htm

*Struggle, Challenge, and Meaning: The Education of a Gifted Child,* by Valerie Bock. Gifted children deserve the same opportunities as other children to test their mettle and emerge victorious, and to experience the rewards of meaningful work.

`http://www.hoagiesgifted.org/enrichment.htm`

*Horizontal Enrichment versus Vertical Acceleration,* by Draper Kauffman, Ed.D. Items with standard 2nd grade vocabulary and standard explanations are unlikely to interest a gifted 2nd grader.

`http://www.hoagiesgifted.org/wish_list.htm`

*Parents Wish List for Educators,* Jean Schweers, Ed.D. "We, the parents of gifted and talented students, wish schools, administrators, and teachers would. . . ."

### Hoagies' Gifted Education Page

`http://www.hoagiesgifted.org/`

This extensive site helps meet the needs of parents and educators of gifted children. Included are articles, research, books, organizations, conferences, online support groups, academic programs, products, and organizations that support gifted education locally, nationally, and globally.

### Exceptional Education Federal Regulations

`http://www.ideapractices.org/lawandregs.htm`

This site posts newly released federal regulations for exceptional children.

### Selective Mutism

`http://www.lib.muohio.edu/edpsych/wwwboard/`
`messages/17.html`

http://www.anxietynetwork.com/spsm.html

### Anxiety Disorders Association of America

`http://www.adaa.org`

### Association for the Advancement of Behavior Therapy

`http://www.aabt.org`

### Selective Mutism Foundation

`http://www.orgsites.com/fl/selectivemutismfoundation`

### Family Village Selective Mutism Page

http://laran.waisman.wisc.edu/fv/www/
lib_selmutism.htm

### Suite 101: Special Education Site

http://www.suite101.com/welcome.cfm/special_education

This site rates the top five Web sites for special education. It also contains current featured articles and links for parents with children in special education.

### American Association of Mental Retardation

http://www.aamr.org

This is an online resource for publications, training, careers, conventions, policies, and resources.

### Bureau for At Risk Youth

http://www.at-risk.com

This is a resource site to help today's youth cope with important issues that face them. It includes an at risk resources directory, an issues forum, a buyer's guide, and a free catalogue order form.

### At-Risk Directed Research and Publications

http://www.ed.gov/offices/OERI/At-Risk/direct1.html

This site outlines successful at-risk programs.

### ADHD/ADD Regulation Site

http://www.ed.gov/offices/OSERS/IDEA/Brief-6.html

This is a Web site that offers access to federal regulations online via GPO access. It contains a browse feature and also contains final regulations on Brief 6 for children with ADD/ADHD—March 1999.

### ADD Assessment

http://www.amenclinic.com.

Dr. Daniel Amen has a fascinating Web site that has a huge source of resources related to ADD/ADHD. One of his books, *Windows Into the ADD Mind,* is great reading for someone interested in the subject.

### Children and Adults with Attention Deficit Disorder (CHADD)

http://www.chadd.com

### ADD Newsletter

http://www.helpforadd.com

In addition to this site, David Rabiner also publishes an online newsletter entitled *ADHD research update*. There is a modest cost for the online research newsletter however David offers free issues for review.

### The ADD/ADHD/LD Links and Resources Page

http://www.angelfire.com/ny/Debsimms/add.html

### ADD Main Table of Contents

http://www3.sympatico.ca/frankk/contents.html

### Fifty Tips on the Classroom Management of Attention Deficit Disorder

http://www3.sympatico.ca/frankk/50class.html

### LD in Depth: ADD/ADHD Resources

http://www.ldonline.org/ld_indepth/add_adhd/
add-adhd.html

### Attention Deficit Disorder in the Classroom

http://www.chadd.org/factsheetpdfs/factsheet4.pdf

### National Attention Deficit Disorder Association

http://www.add.org./

### ADD Warehouse

http://www.addwarehouse.com

1-800-233-9273

### Related Sites:

http://www.sciam.com/1998/0998issue/0998barkley.html
http://www.mentalhealth.com/dis-rs/frs-ch01.html

### ADDHELP-Attention Deficit Disorder-Solutions for Teachers and Parents of ADD/ADHD Kids

http://www.addhelp.com

This site has a lot of great tips as well as information about how to order a really good book on the subject.

### ADD/Parent Site

http://www.med.virginia.edu/medicine/clinical/
pediatrics/devbeh/adhdlin/

This site was created by a teacher who has an ADD-ADHD child. There is a lot of information on this site and is very well worth the time it will take to look it over.

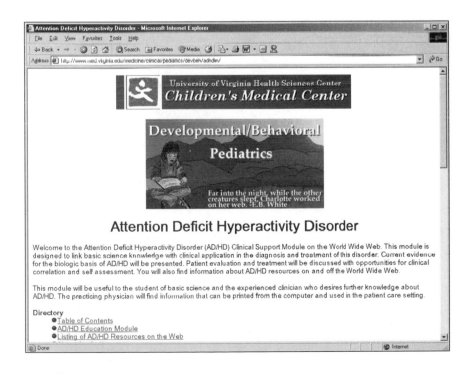

### ADHD/Special Needs Resources: Kids Who Thrive "Outside the Box!"

http://adhd.kids.tripod.com

Grade Level: K–12, Parent & Professional

### Teaching Tips: ADHD

http://www.central.edu/education/REX/adhd.html

This site includes helpful information for dealing with the ADHD student in your classroom, including good teaching tips and strategies for the teacher.

### Adults with Attention Deficit Disorder

Email: adult@maelstrom.stjohns.edu

| | |
|---|---|
| http://yourhealthdaily.com | Daily Health News |
| http://school.discovery.com/ homeworkhelp/bjpinchbeck | Outstanding Kid's Resource Page |
| http://www.nfgcc.org | (National Foundation for Gifted and Creative Children) |
| http://www.studentservices.com/ fastweb/ | Financial Aid Scholarship Search |
| http://www.petersons.com/ | College Applications |
| http://www.ed.gov/pubs/parents | Government Education Publications |
| http://trace.wisc.edu/gofr_web/ handbook.html | Download ADA Handbook |
| ADA-related Information | 800-669-EEOC |
| ADD-ONS | P.O. Box 675, Frankfort, IL 60423 |
| ADDA | 800-487-2282 |
| ADDult News | 2620 Ivy Place, Toledo, OH 43613 |
| ADDvantage | P.O. Box 29972, Thornton, CO 80229 |
| Advocacy, Incorporated | 800-252-9108 |
| Ch.A.D.D. | 800-233-4050 |
| Challenge, Incorporated | P.O. Box 488, West Newbury, MA 01985 |
| Learning Disabilities Association | 412-340-1515 |
| National Center For Law and Learning Disabilities, Incorporated | 301-469-8308 |

### ACT Web Site—Information for Life's Transitions

http://www.act.org

### Closed Captioning Web

`http://www.captions.org`

This site has information accessible to students with hearing impairments, ESL, and other language difficulties. Links to companies that provide non-professional captioning software are available so that, for a relatively small fee, counselors can caption their own educational materials.

### Disability Information and Resources

`http://www.makoa.org`

A directory of many disability resources. This site contains links to general disability resources, newsletters, Web sites on people with disabilities, a disability-solutions page, and current political stances of disability.

### Dyslexia

`http://www.dyslexia.com`

The Gift is an online information center dedicated to the positive side of learning disability as well as to remedial therapies and teaching methods suited to the dyslexic learning style.

### Internet Resources for Special Children

`http://www.irsc.org`

Information for parents, educators, medical professionals, and others who interact with children who have disabilities.

### MedWeb

`http://www.medweb.emory.edu/medweb/default.htm`

Contains links to an array of disability-related information.

### Organizations and Associations Worldwide for Down Syndrome

`http://www.nas.com/downsyn/org.html`

Includes contact information and links, when available, to worldwide associations for Down Syndrome.

### Parent Soup

`http://www.parentsoup.com/edcentral/LD`

Parent Soup is a parenting library about learning disabilities and dyslexia. It contains articles ranging from memory problems to treatment.

### Recording for the Blind and Dyslexic (RFB&D)

http://www.rfbd.org

A national nonprofit organization that serves people who cannot read standard print because of a visual, perceptual, or other physical disability. The organization also offers the nonprofit sale of dictionaries, reference materials, and professional books on computer disk (E-text), and specially adapted tape players/recorders to use with their audio books.

### The Sibling Support Project Home Page

http://www.chmc.org/departmt/sibsupp

Dedicated to the interests of brothers and sisters of people with special health and developmental needs, this site offers information about workshops, existing sibling programs, resources, and SibNet (a list service for siblings of people with special needs.

### National Academy for Child Development (NACD)

http://www.nacd.org

An international organization of parents and professionals dedicated to helping children and adults reach their full potential, NACD designs very specific home educational and therapeutic programs for infants, children, and adults.

### The James Stanfield Publishing Company

http://www.stanfield.com

The most respected library of educational materials available today for students with cognitive challenges, the company provides texts for programs about assertion training, sexuality education, social skills, and working skills.

### UPSIDE!

http://www.telebyte.com/upside/upside.html

### National Organization of Rare Disorders, Inc. (NORD)

http://www.rarediseases.org

NORD is a federation of more than 140 not-for-profit volunteer health organizations serving people with rare disorders and disabilities.

### Kids Together, Inc.

http://www.kidstogether.org

The mission statement of this nonprofit organization is "To promote inclusive communities where all people belong." The site provides helpful information and resources to enhance the quality of life for children and adults with disabilities, and for communities. Businesses can take advantage of the numerous marketing opportunities offered by the Kids Together Day Festival.

### Multicultural Discovery Activities for the Elementary Grades

By Elizabeth Stull. Contains 150 reproducible pages addressing a variety of cultures. MarCo Products 1-800-448-2197

### The School Counselor's Book of Lists

1-800-288-4745. Ask for title code C1293–4.

### Bullying Online

http://www.successunlimited.co.uk
http://www.successunlimited.co.uk/bullycide/child.htm

### More Bullying Sites

http://www.esu3.org/districts/millard/
    south/guid/msguid.html
http://guidance.www.comm.com

### Healthy Oakland Teens Curriculum

http://www.caps.ucsf.edu/curricula/hotcurr.html

The Healthy Oakland Teens curriculum is divided into six teacher-led sessions and eight peer-led sessions available for download.

### Electronic Schoolhouse

http://www.eschoolhouse.com
http://teachnet.com

### Suicide Resources for Teachers

http://www.himh.org.au/response-ability/index.htm

### Employers, Families, and Education

http://www.ed.gov/pubs/EmpFamEd

This site tells how employers can improve education through family-friendly business policies and partnerships with local schools. *The Corporative Imperative: Results and Benefits of Business Involvement in Education* explores how businesses can create strategic education alliances that meet business objectives and promote systemic education change.

## ASSESSMENT AND TESTING RESOURCES

### Consulting Psychologists Press, Inc.

http://www.cpp-db.com/

CPP is the exclusive publisher of the Myers-Briggs Type Indicator. (MBTI), Strong Interest InventoryTM, FIROTM, and the CPITM.

### Keirsey Temperament and Character Web Site

http://www.keirsey.com

This link is for a free test that is very similar to the Myers-Briggs.

### Buros Institute of Mental Measurements

http://www.unl.edu/buros

This site provides professional assistance, expertise, and information to users of commercially published tests. Listed are records of over 10,000 tests and research instruments, including information about ETS tests on microfiche. The site includes a test locator and subject index.

### ERIC/AE Test Locator

http://ericae.net/testcol.htm

This is an updated test locator including ERIC Clearinghouse for assessment and evaluation.

## PARENT EDUCATION

### U.S. Department of Education

http://www.ed.gov/pubs/parents

*Helping Your Child Learn Math . . . Reading . . . History . . . Responsible Behavior*—all these resources are online at the U.S. Department of Education, including a new report, *Simple Things You Can Do to Help a Child Read Well and Independently.*

### American Library Association's site

http://www.ala.org/parentspage

### Family Education Network

http://familyeducation.com/article/
0,1120,1-9834-1,00.html

### Apple Learning Interchange

http://ali.apple.com/

These online handouts contain wonderful topics such as how to complain constructively, the importance of reading, parent and family places online, parents, homework, and computers, preparing your child for the first day of school, and separation anxieties.

## PARENTING WORKSHOPS

### *The Positive Parenting Page*

http://positiveparenting.com/

### *Stephen Glenn and Jane Nelsen's work*

http://www.empoweringpeople.com

### *For Everything on Adolescence*

http://education.indiana.edu/cas/normal.html

### *Step Kit by Dinkmeyer*

http://www.agsnet.com

### *The National PTA*

http://www.pta.org

The National PTA has developed national standards for parent and family involvement in schools.

### *America Goes Back to School*

http://www.ed.gov/Family/agbts

### *ICN Digest*

Email: cpool@ascd.org

*Web Wonders: Engaging Parents and Community in Schools,* compiled by Carolyn R. Pool.

### *Growing Up Drug-Free: A Parent's Guide to Prevention*

http://www.ed.gov/offices/OESE/SDFS/parents_guide

This site includes suggestions on talking with your children effectively, what to do if you think your child might be using drugs, how to teach your child about drugs, where to get information and help, and more.

### *The Connect for Kids Weekly*

http://www.connectforkids.org

This site is a source for the latest news on issues affecting kids and families published by the Benton Foundation.

### Red Ribbon Week Resource

http://www.redribboncoalition.org

### Home and School Institute

http://www.MegaSkillsHSI.org

How do parents rate the teachers of their children? What can schools and teachers learn from parents' answers to questions like "Does this teacher appear to enjoy teaching and believe in what he or she does in school"? Dorothy Rich of the Home and School Institute explores the results of such surveys in her EL article, *What Parents Want from Teachers*.

## MEDIATION RESOURCES/SAFE SCHOOLS

### Conflict Resolution

http://www.bouldenpublishing.com

This site offers free demo conflict resolution interactive CDs to elementary school counselors. This CD runs on both Mac and PC and contains relaxation exercise plus limited demo of interactive material. If interested, send $3.75 to cover shipping to address below. email: jboulden@bouldenpub.com

### A Guide to Safe Schools

http://www.ed.gov/offices/OSERS/OSEP/
    Products/earlywrn.html
http://www.ed.gov/PressReleases/08-1998/violence.html

*Early Warning, Timely Response: A Guide to Safe Schools* was developed at the President's request by the Departments of Justice and Education, in co-operation with the National Association of School Psychologists. It tells what to look for and what to do to prevent violence, how to intervene and get help for troubled children, and how to respond when violent situations occur. (The guide is also available by calling 1-877-4ED-PUBS.)

### NCES Publication Released

http://nces.ed.gov/pubsearch

This report, *Indicators of School Crime and Safety, 1988,* is the first in a series of annual reports on school crime and safety from the Bureau of Justice Statistics and the National Center for Education Statistics. It presents the latest available data on school crime and student safety. The report provides a profile of school crime and safety in the United States and describes the characteristics of the victims of these crimes. It is organized as a series of indicators, with each indicator presenting data on different aspects of school crime and safety. There are five sections to the report: Nonfatal Student Victimization—Student Reports; Violence and Crime at School; Nonfatal Teacher Victimization at School—Teacher Reports; and School Environment. Each section contains a set of indicators that, taken as a whole, describe a distinct aspect of school crime and safety.

### Center for Prevention of School Violence

`http://www.ncsu.edu/cpsv/`

This site offers information, program assistance, and research on school violence prevention. The "Safe Schools Pyramid" offers prevention programs such as "School Resource Officers" and "Conflict Management Peer Mediation."

### Teacher Talk

`http://education.indiana.edu/cas/tt/ttarticles.html`

This site focuses on ways to manage student disruptions. Under "Interventions" click on "Respect" and "Topics for Creating a Peaceful Classroom" for simple steps educators can take to ensure a friendlier and more productive relationship with students.

### NEA Today Online: One Year After the School Shootings

`http://www.nea.org/neatoday`

In the year since the tragic school shootings in Arkansas, Oregon, and Pennsylvania, NEA members nationwide have been working to create schools where all students feel safe. The April edition of *NEA Today Online* synthesizes the latest research.

### NEA Response to Littleton, Colorado

`http://www.nea.org/nr/st990421.html`

This NEA html page posts responses and recommendations for prevention of school violence after the Littleton, Colorado massacre.

### Violence Prevention Resources

`http://www.schoolcounselor.org/content.cfm?L1=4`

A series of publications about preventing violence and taunting in schools.

### Blueprint for Violence Prevention

`http://www.colorado.edu/cspv/blueprints/index.html`

This site is an excellent resource for violence prevention from the Center for the Study and Prevention of Violence (CSPV) and the Colorado Division of Criminal Justice and the Center for Disease Control (CDC). This site identifies ten violence prevention programs which meet high standards in program effectiveness. They include: Midwestern Prevention, Big Brothers—Big Sisters, Functional Family Therapy, Multisystemic Therapy, Nursing Home Visitation, Treatment Foster Care, Quantum Opportunities, Life Skills Training, Paths, and Bullying Prevention.

### Association for School Curriculum Development (ASCD)

`http://www.ascd.org/safeschools/`

This Web site offers resources on violence prevention which includes books and articles.

### Selected ERIC Abstracts on School Violence

- *Reducing School Violence through Conflict Resolution Training*
  NASSP Bulletin v80 n579 p11–18 Apr 1996

- *Taking a Stand Against Violence. Leadership and Responsibility: One School's Quest to Create a Safe Harbor* UMI 1-800-248-0360
- *Drugs and School Violence* Education and Treatment of Children, v20 n3 p263–80 Aug. 1997
- *The Evolution of Violence in Schools* Educational Leadership, v55 n2 p18–20 Oct 1997
- *What is Violence Prevention, Anyway?* Educational Leadership, v54 n8 p31–33 May 1997
- *Protecting Your School and Students: The Safe Schools Handbook* NASSP Bulletin, v80 n579 p44–48 Apr 1996
- *The Art of Safe School Planning* School Administrator, v53 n2 p14–21 Feb 1996
- *Safe School: A Planning Guide for Action. 1995 Edition* California State Department of Education, Sacramento: California State Office of the Attorney General, Sacramento. 174p.: For 1989 edition, see ED 313 815
- *A Guide to Violence Prevention* Educational Leadership, v52 n5 p57–59 Feb 1995
- *Real School Safety Depends upon Safe-Oriented Discipline Policies* EDRS 1-800-443-3742 Ref #ED330028
- *How to Keep Your School and Students Safe. Tips for Principals from NASSP* National Association of Secondary School Principals, Reston, Va. (703-684-3345) Mar 1990 3p.
- *A Study of the Knowledge and Skills of Teachers on School Safety* Nov. 1996 13p.; Paper presented at the Mid-South Education Research Association (Tuscaloosa, AL., November 6, 1996). EDRS 1-800-443-3742 Ref ED402296
- *In Pursuit of Goal Six: A Statewide Initiative to Improve School Safety* Apr 1994 18p.; Paper presented at the Annual Meeting of the American Educational Research Association ( New Orleans, LA, April 4–8, 1994). EDRS 1-800-443-3742 Ref #373453

## HOMESCHOOLING

### Jon's Homeschool Resources Page

`http://www.midnightbeach.com/hs/Welcome.html`

Jon Shemitz keeps his site up-to-date with a variety of resources for homeschoolers, including links to listservs, discussion groups, Web sites, and local and national support groups. The site also contains some full-text articles.

### Homeschool Headlines

`http://www.homeschoolheadlines.com`

A free online publication to support, inform, and empower homeschoolers, this site offers many articles. Some articles offer practical advice about teaching math; others tell success stories. Click on "Controversial Issues" for differing views on the questions: Should There Be a Separation Between School and State? or Should Government Continue Directing Education in America? The site also includes newsletters aimed at homeschoolers in Maryland and Pennsylvania.

### Colleges That Admit Homeschoolers FAQ

`http://learninfreedom.org/colleges_4_hmsc.html`

Here's another page from "School Is Dead; Learn in Freedom!" You've homeschooled your kids and now it's time to think about applying to college. This site lists more than 730 links to colleges and universities that have accepted homeschooled students. Scroll through the list to find information and resources from universities, homeschooling associations, and government agencies.

### Manitoba Homeschool Page

`http://www.flora.org/homeschool-ca/test/index.htm`

Canadians (and others) can try this page, which has the province's rules and regulations for home-based educators, a registration page for "homeschool keypals," a great annotated list of Internet links (including sites originating in the Netherlands and the United Kingdom), and a great quote from Mark Twain: "Don't let school interfere with your education." (This quote itself is also a link to Twain e-texts, including *Huckleberry Finn* and *A Connecticut Yankee*.)

### The National Homeschool Association

`http://www.n-h-a.org`

Based in the United States, this association's site isn't very interactive, but it provides basic information about the association's mission, philosophy, and offerings. An address and telephone number are listed for further details.

### Calvert School

`http://home.calvertschool.org`

An accredited home instruction source long used by United States foreign service personnel, missionaries, and other folks stationed in remote places, this nonprofit organization offers a full nondenominational, nonsectarian curriculum for K–8 students, including advisory teachers, chat rooms, electronic bulletin boards, CD-ROMs, and multimedia resources.

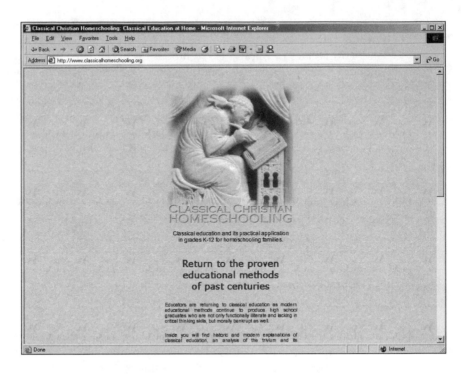

### Christian Homeschooling

`http://www.classicalhomeschooling.org`

By far, the most prominent feature of homeschooling Web sites researched is the Christian faith.

### Rescue 2010

`http://www.nace-cee.org/rescue2010.htm`

Rescue 2010 is a movement that endorses homeschooling for Christian families and promotes seeking "common ground" on controversial issues; seeking "safe-passage" for all K–12 children throughout the system by being spiritually and morally unharmed or academically stunted; and organizing Christians in every school district to become involved in their local schools to oversee and ensure the above objectives.

### Islamic Educational and Muslim Home School Resources

`http://www.muslimhomeschool.com`

Not just the Christian faith is represented in the homeschooling community. This page offers teaching ideas for Muslims and non-Muslims, lists curriculum resources, and sponsors a listserv for all Muslim educators.

## SCHOOL COUNSELING JOURNALS

### *The Journal of Technology in Counseling*

`http://jtc.colstate.edu`

A peer reviewed journal, soon to be published quarterly (July, October, January, and April) through the efforts of the Department of Counseling and Clinical Programs at Columbus State University. JTC is published in a Web-based format and represents an innovative approach to publication not seen in the counseling literature. Submissions will be accepted effective April 1, 1999. *The Journal of Technology in Counseling* publishes articles on all aspects of practice, theory, research, and professionalism related to the use of technology in counselor training and counseling practice. For more information about the journal take a look at the JTC Web site which contains a list of current journal editors, guidelines for authors, and a sample design format to assist authors.

### *Mediation Quarterly*

`http://cgi.jbp.com/JBJournals/mq.html`

### *Counselor Education and Supervision*

`http://www.counseling.org/journals/`

### *Elementary School Guidance and Counseling*

`http://www.counseling.org/journals/`

### *Journal of Humanistic Education and Development*

`http://www.counseling.org/journals/`

### *Journal of Special Education Technology*

`http://jset.unlv.edu`

### *AIDS Education and Prevention*

`http://www.guilford.com/periodicals/jnai.htm`

### *Journal of HIV/AIDS Prevention and Education for Adolescents and Children*

`http://www.haworthpressinc.com`

*Research Navigator Guide: Helping Professions*

## TECHNOLOGY RESOURCES

### ERIC Digest

http://www.ed.gov/databases/ERIC_Digests/
ed347480.html

For ideas on using computers with elementary kids, "Counseling Using Technology with At-Risk Youth" is available free online. The ERIC reference number is ED347480, Dec. '92.

### Counseling and Technology Bibliography

http://www.schoolcounselor.com/bibliogr.htm

### Tools for Schools; Families and Schools Together

http://www.ed.gov/pubs/ToolsforSchools/fast.html

## Addictions/Dual Diagnosis

### SUBSTANCE ABUSE

### Substance Abuse and Treatment of State and Federal Prisoners

http://www.ojp.usdoj.gov/bjs/abstract/satsfp97.htm

Released on January 5, this new study by the Bureau of Justice Statistics (BJS) reports a rise in the proportion of state inmates who used drugs (including alcohol) in the month before their arrest and an increase in the use by federal inmates within prisons between 1990 and 1997. In the same period, the proportions of state inmates receiving drug abuse treatment fell from 24.5 percent in 1991 to 9.7 percent in 1997, and the numbers of inmates in treatment in federal prisons fell from 15.7 percent to 9.2 percent. Analysts attribute these figures to both a new awareness by police and the court system toward offender drug use and the exploding prison population, which has doubled since it reached 1.8 million in 1981. Available in.pdf or ASCII format, the report contains data tables on "prior alcohol and drug abuse by types of offender characteristics," as well as the types of treatment and programs in prisons. A press release, spreadsheets in.zip format, and related data sets are also available.

### College on Problems of Drug Dependence (CPDD)

http://views.vcu.edu/cpdd

CPDD serves as an interface among governmental, industrial, and academic communities maintaining liaisons with regulatory and research agencies as well as educational, treatment, and prevention facilities in the drug abuse field. It also functions as a collaborating center of the World Health Organization.

### Drug Strategies

`http://www.drugstrategies.org`

Drug Strategies is a nonprofit research institute promoting more effective approaches to the nation's drug problems by supporting private and public initiatives that reduce the demand for drugs through prevention, education, treatment, law enforcement, and community coalitions.

### Center for Education and Drug Abuse Research (CEDAR)

`http://cedar.pharmacy.pitt.edu`

CEDAR serves to elucidate the factors contributing to the variation in the liability to drug abuse and determine the developmental pathways culminating in drug abuse outcome, normal outcome, and psychiatric/behavioral disorder outcome. CEDAR is a consortium between the University of Pittsburgh and St. Francis Medical Center.

### The American Council for Drug Education

`http://www.drughelp.org`

This site contains information on drugs and other harmful substances and contains a database of more then 1,200 treatment programs. It also covers topics like alcohol in the workplace, drugs and pregnancy, and talking to a child about marijuana.

### International Narcotics Research Conference (INRC)

`http://www.inrcworld.org`

The International Narcotics Research Conference is an annual meeting designed to bring together drug abuse researchers from around the world. A diverse group of scientists present their latest results on the basic mechanisms of narcotic drug action. Important advances in molecular, cellular, and behavioral aspects of narcotic action are presented and discussed. Attendance is open and further information can be obtained from:

### The National Center on Addiction and Substance Abuse at Columbia University (CASA)

`http://www.casacolumbia.org`

The National Center on Addiction and Substance Abuse at Columbia University (CASA) is a resource for research on addiction and substance abuse. It provides access to information, research, and commentary on tobacco, alcohol, and drug abuse issues including prevention, treatment, and cost data.

### National Clearinghouse for Drug and Alcohol Information/Prevention Online

`http://www.health.org`

The National Clearinghouse for Alcohol and Drug Information (NCADI) is the information service of the Center for Substance Abuse Prevention of the U.S. Department of Health and Human Services. NCADI is the world's largest resource for current information and materials about alcohol and other drugs. The National Clearinghouse for Alcohol and Drug Information is a site which contains: missing children links, funding opportunities, treatment organizations, information on federal workplace, drug testing programs, laboratories for urine drug testing, resource for runaways, Internet links, and publications from NCADI. This Web site contains links to other Internet sites related to substance abuse information.

### National Association of Alcoholism and Drug Abuse Counselors

`http://www.naadac.org`

NAADAC's mission is to provide leadership in the alcoholism and drug abuse counseling profession by building new visions, effecting change in public policy, promoting criteria for effective treatment, encouraging adherence to ethical standards, and ensuring professional growth for alcoholism and drug abuse counselors.

### The Office of National Drug Control Policy

`http://www.ncjrs.org/htm/toc.htm`

The Office of National Drug Control Policy (ONDCP) was established by Act of Congress in 1988 and is organized within the Executive Office of the President. ONDCP is authorized to develop and coordinate the policies, goals, and objectives of the nation's drug control program for reducing the use of illicit drugs. ONDCP engages in activities that both meet the requirements of its authorization and represent the values and commitments of the President and its Director.

### Robert Wood Johnson Foundation Substance Abuse Policy Research Program

`http://www.phs.bgsm.edu/sshp/rwj/rwj.htm`

Research Navigator Guide: Helping Professions

The site includes project summaries, grant application information, and links to other sites relating to substance abuse. The goal of the program is to identify, analyze, and evaluate policies regarding tobacco, alcohol, and drug abuse.

### The Substance Abuse and Mental Health Data Archive (SAMHDA)

`http://www.icpsr.umich.edu/SAMHDA`

SAMHDA's purpose is to increase the utilization of substance abuse and mental health databases, thereby encouraging their use to understand and assess the extent of alcohol, drug abuse, and mental health disorders, and the nature and impact of related treatment systems. Based at the University of Michigan's Inter-university Consortium for Political and Social Research (ICPSR).

### The UCLA Drug Abuse Research Center (DARC)

`http://www.medsch.ucla.edu/som/npi/DARC/search.html`

The Drug Abuse Research Center (DARC) is a diverse research organization that investigates psychosocial and epidemiological issues pertaining to drug use and conducts evaluations of interventions for drug dependence.

The group's portfolio of studies has provided findings that have improved the understanding of the complex nature of drug use and dependence. DARC findings have been useful in developing more effective strategies for dealing with drug-related problems through prevention, treatment, and criminal justice approaches.

### Web of Addictions

`http://www.well.com/user/woa`

The Web of Addictions is dedicated to providing accurate information about alcohol and other drug addictions. The Web of Addictions was developed for several reasons: concern about the pro drug use messages in some Web sites and in some use groups; concern about the appalling extent of misinformation about abused drugs on the Internet, particularly on some usenet news groups; and the desire to provide a resource for teachers, students, and others who need factual information about abused drugs.

### National Institute on Drug Abuse (NIDA)

`http://www.nida.nih.gov`

This Web site contains recent studies funded by NIDA, research on tobacco, research on economic costs of alcohol and drug abuse in the United States, latest survey results, research reports on addiction, NIDA information fax, a bi-monthly newsletter, materials for teachers, scientists, health practitioners, and students, subscription to mailing lists, science drug education, constituent organizations, grantees, government sites of interest, and site searches.

`http://www.nida.nih.gov/Prevention/Prevopen.html`

The government has officially embraced a new approach to drug abuse, emphasizing both counseling and medical treatment of addiction. The National Institute on Drug Abuse issued two treatment manuals that take counselors and other professionals step-by-step through a drug treatment program. "For the first time the strategy is what I feel to be a science-based strategy," NIDA director Dr. Alan Leshner told a conference of drug abuse professionals.

### Children of Alcoholics

`http://www.hazelden.org`

### The Recovery Net

`http://members.aol.com/r2135/index.htm`

The Recovery Network, an organization whose mission is to provide "prevention and recovery information, interaction and support concerning substance use and abuse, addiction to alcohol, tobacco and other drugs, and behavioral and mental health problems," maintains this site which digests the latest news from over 1,400 sources (according to site). At this time, *Recovery Network News* contains approximately one week's worth of article digests from such sources as the *Wall Street Journal, USA Today,* the *Washington Post, Reuters,* the *New York Times,* and *Investors Business Daily.* The news can be downloaded as a Microsoft Word file, and interested readers can also subscribe to a weekly email version.

### Center on Substance Abuse for Teens

http://www.wholefamily.com/kidteencenter/
thecenter.html

Check out the fantastic new Substance Abuse Center.

### Manual of Therapeutics for Addictions

http://www.josseybass.com/Corporate/Website/
Objects/Products/0,9049,106437,00.html

A practical guide to the effective diagnosis and treatment of alcohol and drug addictive disorders. Edited by Norman Miller, University of Illinois, Mark S. Gold, University of Florida, and David E. Smith, American Society of Addiction Medicine.

### Collegiate Alcohol and Other Drug Use

http://www.lasalle.edu/~chapman

### Center for Education and Drug Abuse Research (University of Pittsburgh)

http://cedar.pharmacy.pitt.edu

### Phoenix House

http://www.phoenixhouse.org

This New York nonprofit substance abuse service organization has established a site with referral information, its treatment philosophy and other material.

### Addiction Psychiatry: Current Diagnosis and Treatment

`http://www.wiley.com/psychiatry/norman.htm`

This site is authored by Norman S. Miller, MD, University of Illinois at Chicago.

### Buprenorphine: Combating Drug Abuse with a Unique Opioid

`http://www.wiley.com/psychiatry/cowan.htm`

This site is edited by Alan Cowan, Temple University School of Medicine, and John W. Lewis, University of Bristol, United Kingdom.

### Journal of Drug Education

`http://www.baywood.com/search/`
`PreviewJournal.asp?qsRecord=13`

### Mental Health Net

`http://mentalhelp.net/`

### Hope and Healing Web Chronicles

http://www.hopeandhealing.com/

Hope and Healing Web Chronicles is a healing journal focusing on the spiritual journeys and personal transformations possible for the family affected by alcoholism and addiction. The site includes insights, observations and musings of the Web publisher, W. Waldo; articles by well-known published authors; and numerous links and descriptions of Web sites related to alcoholism. This extensive site is a great place to look for support for alcoholism.

### Twelve Step Cyber Cafe

http://www.12steps.org/

The goal of this site is to help visitors find information about addiction, as well as the help that is available. Visitors that are new to recovery might find the Menuboard of Recovery helpful. This site provides a chat room for its visitors to share their experiences with each other, and a bulletin board which provides some helpful information on local meetings throughout the world. This site is frequently updated and simple to navigate.

### Common Sense

http://www.pta.org/commonsense/

Common Sense provides strategies for raising drug- and alcohol free children. This site contains substance abuse prevention facts, positive parenting tips, and family prevention activities. Information is targeted toward parents of young children, but may be useful to counselors and community leaders. An informative and attractive site.

### Parallel Paths of Recovery

http://www.parallel-paths.org

Dual Diagnosis Support Group for Individuals diagnosed with a mental/emotional illness as well as an addictive disorder and their Significant Others. This site provides, email lists, chat, forums, and links for all forms of dual diagnosis.

### Christians in Recovery

http://www.christians-in-recovery.com

Members work to regain and maintain balance and order in their lives through active discussion of the Twelve Steps, the Bible, and experiences in their own recovery. The only purpose of Christians in Recovery is to provide information and referral for anyone who desires to recover from abuse, family dysfunction, addictions of alcohol, drugs, food, and pornography. Christians in Recovery does not engage in providing individualized professional services or counseling.

### Recovery Online

```
http://www.onlinerecovery.org
```

A comprehensive listing of self-help, recovery groups online, including twelve-step groups, religious groups, as well as secular groups. This is a great place to begin a search!

### Al-Anon/Alateen

```
http://www.Al-Anon-Alateen.org
```

Al-Anon (and Alateen for younger members) is a worldwide organization that offers a self-help recovery program for families and friends of alcoholics. The listings of the Twelve Steps, Traditions, and Concepts of Al-Anon are helpful for those who are seeking more information on the goals and objectives of this program. Also included are an approved literature section, a discussion forum, and a guide for professionals.

### Alcoholics Victorious

```
http://av.iugm.org/
```

A Christian oriented twelve-step support group for recovering alcoholics, the site includes information and referrals, literature, phone support, conferences, support group meetings, and the organization's newsletter. An informative FAQ is provided for new visitors.

### Big Book of Alcoholics Anonymous

```
http://www.recovery.org/aa/bigbook/ww/
```

An indexed and fully searchable copy of the main text of Alcoholics Anonymous. Also online is the unpublished, original manuscript of the book.

### Santa Barbara County Alcohol and Drug Program

```
http://www.silcom.com/~sbadp/
```

### Connecticut Clearinghouse

```
http://www.ctclearinghouse.org/
```

*Research Navigator Guide: Helping Professions*

Connecticut Clearinghouse is a resource center for information about alcohol, tobacco, and other drugs. A fact sheet answers many common questions in a easy-to-read manner, the research page keeps you up-to-date on certain projects, and the message page allows one to interact with others. The Connecticut Clearinghouse provides free information to Connecticut residents about chemical dependency and related topics such as mental illness, violence, fetal alcohol syndrome, and suicide.

### Kathleen Sciacca

http://www.erols.com/ksciacca/

This site is designed to provide information and resources for service providers, consumers, and family members who are seeking assistance and/or education in the field of co-occurring mental illness, drug addiction and/or alcoholism in various combinations.

### HabitSmart

http://www.cts.com/crash/habtsmrt/

This Web site has been constructed to provide an abundance of information about addictive behavior, including theories of habit endurance and habit change as well as tips for effectively managing problematic habitual behavior. Includes the Self-Scoring Alcohol Check-Up, an online questionnaire for people concerned about their alcohol consumption. Many of the articles are written by Robert W. Westermeyer, Ph.D.

### InfoSite

http://www.drugs.indiana.edu/

An information clearinghouse of prevention, technical assistance, and information about alcohol, tobacco, and other drugs. This site includes searchable databases (including an online dictionary of street drug slang), more than 1,000 full-text documents, more than 2,000 links to prevention sites and Web pages, and a library of more than 200 educational photos of drugs available for free download. Although this site provides a great deal of information, it is not regularly updated.

### Internet Alcohol Recovery Center

http://www.med.upenn.edu/~recovery/

This site provides information for both consumers and professionals. Highlights of this site include a chat room, information on current research, articles, and a directory of clinics/hospitals. A simple layout makes navigation easy.

### Lynn's Recovery Site

`http://www.geocities.com/dragons_silver_rose5150`

This site is dedicated to those interested in recovery programs based on the Twelve Steps of Alcoholics Anonymous (AA). Since the author's personal experience is with the program of Alcoholics Anonymous, most of the material presented is based on the program of AA. This site is frequently updated.

### National Association for Christian Recovery

`http://www.nacronline.com`

Especially helpful for clients struggling with spiritual or faith-related issues that complicate recovery, this site contains many articles, meditations, forums, and other resources, and is frequently updated.

### Arizona Smokers Helpline

`http://www.ashline.org`

A very large resource for smoking and tobacco related links. This site's library of links is divided up into 8 categories and provides many choices within each. We found it fairly easy to use, but it lacks its own content on tobacco and related topics.

### Secular Organizations for Sobriety

`http://www.unhooked.com/`

The Secular Organizations for Sobriety (SOS) is an alternative, recovery method for those alcoholics or drug addicts who are uncomfortable with the spiritual content of widely available twelve-step programs. It is a rich resource, but the home page is very busy with navigation options and graphics. A helpful FAQ answers questions in a direct manner about the organization and what it's all about.

### SMART Recovery

`http://www.smartrecovery.org/`

SMART Recovery is an abstinence-based, not-for-profit organization with a self-help program for people having problems with drinking and using. This frequently updated site provides a broad overview of what the organization is about. It also contains several primers and manuals concerning alcoholism.

### Sobriety and Recovery Resources

`http://www.recoveryresources.org`

Loading time is lengthy for this huge list of resources for every aspect of recovery. Resources are organized for easy navigation.

### The Royal College of Psychiatrists 'Help is at Hand' Leaflet Series University of Exeter

`http://www.rcpsych.ac.uk/info/help/index.htm`

The University of Exeter is pleased to be able to publish in full the Royal College of Psychiatrists' 'Help is at Hand' Series. The first leaflet was published seven years ago and the topics covered are continually expanding. Over four million leaflets have now been produced by the College.

### Gift of Serenity

`http://www.laserbuddy.com/recover/`

An Al-Anon member's personal story, this site contains touching and inspiring sections on "Acceptance, Courage, Wisdom, and Hope." An excellent resource for those who are recovering from the effects of someone else's drinking problem, this site lists links to other related sites.

### Recovery Net

`http://members.aol.com/r2135/`

This site contains links to twelve-step programs such as Alcoholics Anonymous and to alternative programs like Rational Recovery. It is also helpful in finding discussion groups, therapists, and treatment facilities, although it needs to be updated more often.

### Close to Home Online

`http://www.thirteen.org/closetohome/`

This Web companion to the PBS program "Moyers on Addiction: Close to Home" offers more than just a synopsis of the TV series. You can find information about the effects of illegal drugs, a debate among experts about drug-related issues, advice, and listings of resources to combat illegal drug use. This site also features Overboard, a thirteen-issue soap opera comic book directed at teenagers.

### AlcoWeb

http://www.alcoweb.com/

An informative site for laypeople as well as professionals, AlcoWeb's high-lights include a glossary, prevention and health information, and related re-sources. Text is available in French and English.

### Grant Me the Serenity . . .

http://open-mind.org

A list of recovery links, quotes, and affirmations for various forms of ad-diction, this site includes religious, secular, and twelve-step groups as well as links to general recovery or addiction-related sites. Resources are orga-nized by type of addiction with a brief description. Original graphics make this an attractive site.

### Substance Abuse

http://substanceabuse.miningco.com/

With a focus on drug addiction, this site provides lots of information for both intervention and treatment. Their frequent articles are thoughtful and obviously well-researched. With an abound of helpful links throughout the Web page, this is a great source for information.

### Dual Recovery Anonymous Twelve-Step Program

http://dualrecovery.org/dra/

This site is very comprehensive, containing twenty-one pages. Their home page and Preamble page explain DRA's purposes, values, and philosophy. Additional pages describe their twelve steps; their twelve traditions; answer frequently asked questions; describe their meeting formats; and list where their groups are currently located. The site also includes a discussion fo-rum page, a chat room, and a page set up to conduct an online meeting. The site also includes a recovery gift shop, links to three bookstores, and search pages, for both links to other recovery sites, and other links. Their newsletter is also available through this site. Unique links include a page linking the user to various games, and a jukebox.

### Do It Now Foundation

http://www.doitnow.org/

America's drug information connection, this foundation has been devel-oping innovative publications and education materials on substance abuse, alcoholism & related health since 1968. Currently their site archives the entire roster of educational publications in these areas. It is especially comprehensive in detailing resources about "street" drugs.

### The Big Page of Information for Survivors

`http://www.fiber.net/users/jeffglo/nik.htm`

Contains links of interest for survivors of incest, child abuse, ritual abuse, drug addiction, and those diagnosed with Multiple Personality Disorder (Dissociation). This site was created by a survivor of sexual, emotional, physical, and ritual abuse.

## ADULT CHILDREN OF ALCOHOLICS INFORMATION

### Recovery.org

`http://www.recovery.org/acoa/acoa.html`

This site gives very basic information on adult children of alcoholics. This resource is limited, but it might be of use to point adult children of alcoholics in the right direction.

### Cocaine Anonymous

`http://www.ca.org/`

A fellowship of men and women who share their experience, strength and hope with each other so that they may solve their common problem and help others to recover from their addiction. The only requirement for membership is a desire to stop using cocaine and all other mind-altering substances. There are no dues or fees for membership.

### Instituto para el Estudio de las Adicciones

`http://www.ieanet.com`

The Instituto para el Estudio de las Adicciones is an NGO located in Spain. It is the first Spanish Web site designed to prevent drug addiction. Visitors can find information about drugs, how to talk with children, a calendar of events, who is who, HIV, and more. All text is in Spanish. Loading time is lengthy.

### Jewish Alcoholics, Chemically Dependent Persons and Significant Others

`http://www.jacsweb.org/`

An Internet recovery resource site for Jews and their families whose lives have been affected by alcohol and drugs. The site lists retreats (mostly based in the NYC area), and provides links to local support groups. Other resources are planned for this easy to navigate site.

### Marijuana Anonymous

`http://www.marijuana-anonymous.org/`

Marijuana Anonymous is a fellowship of men and women who share the same experience of addiction. The only requirement for membership is a desire to stop using marijuana. This site contains membership information and pamphlets.

### Minnesota Recovery Page

`http://www.lakeweb1.com/mrp/`

This site provides contact information for various twelve-step groups and recovery resources. An AA meeting directory for much of Minnesota is included.

### Moderation Management

`http://www.moderation.org/`

A recovery program and national support group network for people who have made the healthy decision to reduce their drinking and make other positive lifestyle changes. Provides membership information, a national list of MM support groups, an MM mailing list, chat, and related literature for sale.

### Narcotics Anonymous

`http://www.wsoinc.com/`

Provides some basic information about the Fellowship of Narcotics Anonymous. This site can be helpful in contacting with NA in or near your community.

### Recovery Resources

`http://www.naturesgift.com/recov.htm`

This site contains many Al-Anon, AA, and other twelve-step resources. The author is in the process of recovery, and has created this site as an attempt to give back some of what she has been given. Broken images become distracting.

### Women for Sobriety, Inc.

`http://www.womenforsobriety.org`

Women for Sobriety, Inc. (WFS) is a nonprofit organization dedicated to helping women overcome alcoholism and other addictions. The New Life program helps achieve sobriety and sustain ongoing recovery. A broad overview of the organization is provided, including special reports on the 1997 WFS Conference, WFS Group info, and the WFS bookstore.

### Addiction Resource Guide

`http://www.addictionresourceguide.com`

Addiction Resource Guide is an online directory of inpatient and outpatient treatment facilities. The site has included information about addictions and how the layperson or professional can find the appropriate treatment options. To make navigation easier, resources are divided into appropriate categories. A brief description is provided for each resource listed.

### Recovery Anonymous

`http://www.mlode.com/~ra/`

The author shares his personal experience of recovery. He includes information on all aspects of addictions and how these addictions interact. The inconsistent layout interferes with navigation.

### Recovery Poetry Spa

`http://www.geocities.com/HotSprings/Spa/1416/`

This site features poetry about abuse, addictions, and recovery from them. It invites additional submissions from others. Additional links to recovery and general poetry sites are included.

### National Association of Addiction Treatment Providers

`http://www.naatp.org/`

National Association of Addiction Treatment Providers is dedicated to raising public awareness of addiction as a treatable disease and securing adequate reimbursement for treatment programs. This site is directed toward professional development and membership education. They offer the opportunity to apply for membership or request further information. Laypersons may not benefit significantly from this site.

### Illusion of Drugs

`http://www.donparker.com/`

Entertaining magician with an anti-drug message Don Parker, a former addict, has created a page with some information, moderate self-promotion, and lots of entertainment for the technical savvy with the latest plug-ins. A strong message is presented, but little information joins it.

## BEHAVIORAL DISORDERS

### ODD

`http://www.conductdisorders.com`

Try this Web site for more information on ODD and other conduct disorders.

### National Center of PTSD (Post Traumatic Stress Disorder)

`http://www.ncptsd.org`

Available on this site are research and education on PTSD, training opportunities, and information for victims, trauma survivors, clinicians, researchers, and students.

### The Something Fishy Web site on Eating Disorders

`http://www.something-fishy.org`

This site contains updates for information, Q & A, motivations for recovery, book recommendations, chatroom connections, and treatment options.

### Cyberpsych Anxiety Disorders Page

`http://www.cyberpsych.org/anxdisor/anxiety.htm`

This meta-site has links to a variety of anxiety disorders including panic disorders, childhood phobias, and PTSD.

### Anxiety Panic Internet Resources (tAPir)

`http://www.algy.com/anxiety`

Excellent resource for relaxation techniques, articles, diagnosis, prevention, links, and databases.

### Bipolar Disorders Information Web Site

`http://www.mhsource.com/bipolar`

Online question and answer forum sponsored by Charles W. Bowden, M.D. and Alan Swann, M.D. the first Tuesday of each month from 10 to 11 P.M. (Eastern time). This site is operated by the Continuing Medical Education, Inc.

### Dual Diagnosis

`http://www.toad.net/~arcturus/dd/main.htm`

This resource page for treatment providers working with co-occurring disorders (MH/SA) contains NOVAADAC (Northern Region of the Virginia Association of Alcoholism and Drug Abuse Counselors) newsletter, DSM-IV Axis II personality disorders, a bookstore, and a colleagues page.

### Dual Diagnosis Credentialed Listserv

`To subscribe email:Listserv@maelstrom.stjohns.edu`

The text of your message should read: subscribe DUALDIAG <your full name>

### Dual Diagnosis Web Site

`http://www.erols.com/ksciacca`

Sciacca is comprehensive service development for mental illness, drug addiction and alcoholism (MIDAA). This site is designed to provide information and resources for service providers, consumers, and family members seeking assistance and education in this field.

### Dual Diagnosis Online Dictionary of Mental Health

`http://www.human-nature.com/odmh/dual.html`

Sciacca hosts this Web site for co-occurring mental illness and substance disorders. Complete articles and chapters may be read and downloaded. Also included are a search engine and mailing lists.

### For Today's Families (With Children and Adolescents With Brain Disorders)

`http://www.nami.org/youth/dualdigf.htm`

Fact page containing information on recovery for substance abuse and brain disorders (mental illness) as well as ADHD, depression, and bipolar disorder. Good information for families with adolescents.

## PHYSICAL CONDITIONS

### Teen Pregnancy Report

`http://aspe.hhs.gov/hsp/teenp/97-98rpt.htm`

Recently released online, this document, introduced in January, 1997, by the U.S. Department of Health and Human Services is the first annual report on the progress of the National Strategy to Prevent Teen Pregnancy. The report does contain some good news—teen birth rates have decreased nationally and in all states since 1991, falling twelve percent nationally and sixteen percent or more in seventeen states. The report contains statistics and analysis of teen birth and pregnancy rates, by age and race. It also details the strategies and partnerships forged by the HHS to continue this encouraging trend. Appendixes include Teenage Birth Rates in the United States, National and State Trends, 1990–96, an overview of various HHS teen pregnancy provision programs, and Teen Parent Provisions by State.

### Teen Pregnancy

`http://aspe.hhs.gov/hsp/teenp/intro.htm`

The National Campaign to Prevent Teen Pregnancy has a very comprehensive site from parent brochures to resources they recommend. It may lead you in the direction of a curriculum. There are also awareness week materials for May.

### American Foundation for AIDS Research

`http://www.amfar.org`

The American Foundation for AIDS Research (AmFAR) is the nation's leading nonprofit organization dedicated to the support of AIDS research (both basic biomedical and clinical research), education for AIDS prevention, and sound AIDS-related public policy development.

### Health On the Net Foundation

`http://www.hon.ch`

Health On the Net Foundation is a nonprofit organization whose mission is to build and support the international health and medical community on the Internet and World Wide Web, so that the potential benefits of this new communications medium may be realized by individuals, medical professionals, and healthcare providers. HON site includes a complete list of hospitals on the World Wide Web, Internet medical support communities (listservers, newsgroups, and FAQs), medical sites, and search engines.

### HIV InSite

http://hivinsite.ucsf.edu

HIV InSite is a project of the University of California, San Francisco, AIDS Program at San Francisco General Hospital, and the UCSF Center for AIDS Prevention Studies, which are programs of the UCSF AIDS Research Institute.

### JAMA HIV/AIDS Information Center

http://www.ama~assn.org/special/hiv/hivhome.htm

The JAMA HIV/AIDS Information Center is an easy-to-use, interactive collection of useful and high-quality resources for physicians, other health professionals, and the public.

### Medscape

http://www.medscape.com

This is a new, free Web site for health professionals and interested consumers. Practice-oriented information is peer-reviewed and edited by thought leaders in AIDS, infectious diseases, urology, and surgery. Highly-structured articles and full-color graphics are supplemental with stored literature searches and annotated links to relevant Internet resources. From SCP Communications, Inc., one of the world's leading publishers of medical journals and medical education programs.

## VIOLENCE AND TRAUMA

### The Beck Specialized Treatment Assessment Inventory for Adolescents (BSTAI-A) Research Edition

Email: BeckAssociates@susquehanna-institute.com
http://www.susquehanna-institute.com

This instrument has been used by counselors, psychologists, psychiatrists, juvenile justice, and family and children service professionals, as well as school professionals in various pilots. In a relatively non-threatening and open-ended manner, this protocol asks the questions in a way that allows the interview to access such things as the experiencing of, participating in, witnessing of, or being victimized by such things as physical violence or other forms of trauma.

### Victims' Rights

http://www.ojp.usdoj.gov/ovc/new/directions

This recent report from the U.S. Department of Justice (USDOJ) Office for Victims of Crime (OVC) outlines a comprehensive plan for improving the rights of and services for crime victims in the United States While making some sixty-eight recommendations for improvement, the report also notes the advances that have been made in recent years, highlighting some of the hundreds of "innovative public policy initiatives and community partnerships that are revolutionizing the treatment of crime victims in America today." Users may download the full report in ASCII or .pdf format or view individual chapters in HTML, ASCII or .pdf formats.

## CHILD ABUSE

### The National Victim Center/Child Abuse Bibliography

http://www.ncjrs.org/txtfiles/163390.txt

### Higher Education Center Against Violence and Abuse

http://www.mincava.umn.edu

## SUICIDE/DEATH/DYING

### Crisis, Grief and Healing: Men and Women

http://www.webhealing.com

### Suicide Facts

http://www.nimh.nih.gov/research/suifact.htm

## PREVENTION SITES

### Substance Abuse Treatment Facility Locator

http://findtreatment.samhsa.gov

This site offers a database providing a listing of federal, state, local, and private providers of alcoholism, drug abuse treatment, and prevention services by city, state, territory, and zip code.

*Research Navigator Guide: Helping Professions*

### Media Campaign in Action

http://www.mediacampaign.org/index.html

National youth anti-drug campaign.

### Project Know

http://www.projectknow.com/

### Society for Prevention Research

http://www.oslc.org/spr/sprhome.html

The focus of this society is broadly defined and concerned with the problems pertaining to the prevention of drug and alcohol abuse and associated social maladjustment, crime, and behavior disorders.

### Project CRAFT

http://www.unm.edu/~craft

Project CRAFT, as part of the Research Division at The University of New Mexico Center on Alcoholism, Substance Abuse, and Addictions (UNM-CASAA), involves several treatment outcome studies designed to teach skills to help loved ones of resistant substance abusers convince the users to accept treatment for their drug or alcohol problems.

### PREVLINE: Prevention Online at the National Clearinghouse for Alcohol and Drug Information (NCADI)

http://www.samhsa.gov

PREVLINE is the name of the NCADI's multi-faceted online information activity. NCADI services include an information services staff equipped to respond to the public's alcohol, tobacco, and illicit drug (ATID) inquiries; the distribution of free ATID materials, including fact sheets, brochures, pamphlets, posters, and video tapes from an inventory of over 1,000 items; customized annotated bibliographies from alcohol and other drug databases consisting of over 36,000 records; a Prevention Materials Database (PMD); and Federal grant announcements and application kits for prevention programs, treatment, and research funding opportunities.

### National Inhalant Prevention Coalition

`http://www.inhalants.org`

Synergies, a nonprofit corporation founded by Harvey J. Weiss and based in Austin, Texas, established the National Inhalant Prevention Coalition (NIPC) in 1992. The NIPC grew from a state-wide prevention project in Texas called the Texas Prevention Partnership which began in 1990. NIPC is a public-private effort to promote awareness and recognition of the problem of inhalant use. NIPC is funded in part by the Robert Wood Johnson Foundation and is led by Synergies.

### American Academy of Addiction Psychiatry

`http://www.aaap.org`

The American Academy of Addiction Psychiatry was formed to promote excellence clinical practice in addiction psychiatry; educate the public to influence public policy regarding addictive illness; promote accessibility of quality treatment for all patients; provide continuing education for professionals in the field of addiction psychiatry; disseminate new information in the field of addiction psychiatry; and encourage research on the etiology, prevention, identification, and treatment of the addictions.

### American Society of Addiction Medicine

http://www.asam.org

The nation's medical specialty society is dedicated to educating physicians and improving the treatment of individuals suffering from alcoholism or other addictions.

### Center for Alcohol and Addiction Studies

http://center.butler.brown.edu

The Center's mission is to promote the identification, prevention, and effective treatment of alcohol and other drug use problems in our society through research, publications, education, and training.

### Center for Prevention Research at the University of Kentucky

http://www.uky.edu/RGS/PreventionResearch/
welcome.html

The Center for Prevention Research at the University of Kentucky was established in October, 1987, with funding from the National Institute on Drug Abuse. It was the first such center funded by NIDA.

### Growing Up Drug-Free: A Parent's Guide to Prevention

http://www.ed.gov/offices/OESE/SDFS/parents_guide

This site includes suggestions for talking with your children effectively, what to do if you think your child might be using drugs, how to teach your child about drugs, where to get information and help, and more.

### The Centers for Disease Control and Prevention's (CDC) National Prevention Information Network (NPIN)

http://www.cdcnpin.org

CDC's National Prevention Information Network is designed to facilitate sharing of HIV/AIDS, STD, and TB information and resources.

### National Association of State Alcohol and Drug Abuse Directors (NASADAD)

http://www.nasadad.org/

This site links to conference announcements, community anti-drug coalitions and treatment innovations and initiations.

### *Safe and Drug Free Schools Program*

http://www.ed.gov/offices/OESE/SDFS

## TREATMENT STUDIES

### *Drug Abuse Treatment Outcome Study (DATOS)*

http://www.datos.org

The Drug Abuse Treatment Outcome Study (DATOS) is NIDA's third national evaluation of treatment effectiveness. It is based on over 10,000 admissions during 1991–1993 to ninety-six community-based treatment programs in eleven large United States cities.

## SUPPORT GROUPS

### *Eating Disorder Support Groups*

http://www.hazelden.com

Overeaters Anonymous (OA) is based on the principles of AA.

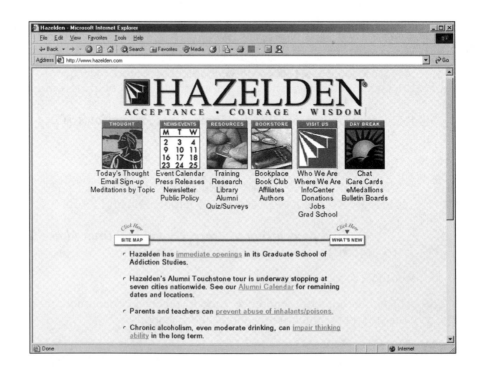

### Rational Recovery (RR) Support Group

http://rational.org/

RR was developed by Jack and Lois Trimpey. Jack has tended to focus on alcoholism and drug addiction. Lois has written mostly about food addictions. Evolved from RET.

### Smart Recovery

http://www.smartrecovery.org/

This is a self management and recovery Web site featuring online recovery meetings Monday and Friday at 10:00 P.M. EST.

## Clinical Psychology/Mental Health

### MENTAL HEALTH SITES

#### BeckNet

http://www.susquehanna-institute.com

#### American Counseling Association

http://www.counseling.org.

This site is a must for all counselors! It contains current information on conferences, resources, books, and listservs.

#### Inter Psych

http://www.shef.ac.uk/~psyc/InterPsych/inter.html

#### SEPI

http://www.cyberpsych.org/sepi

This site is run by the Society for the Exploration of Psychotherapy Integration

#### The Gestalt Therapy Page

http://www.gestalt.org/index.htm

#### American Psychoanalytic Association

http://apsa.org

### Albert Ellis Institute

http://www.rebt.org

### Behavior Online

http://behavior.net

### Radical Psychology Network

http://www.radpsynet.org

### Association for the Advancement of Gestalt Therapy

http://www.aagt.org

### Index of Health

http://www.chebucto.ns.ca/Health

### Psychodrama

http://pages.nyu.edu/~as245/AITG

### The Focusing Institute

http://www.focusing.org

### Ecopsychology, Theory, and Practice

http://www.well.com/user/suscon/esalen/ecopsyche.html

### Art Therapy

http://www.arttherapy.org/

### Self-Psychology Page

http://www.selfpsychology.org

### Personality & Consciousness

http://www.wynja.com/personality/theorists.html

Sketches of leading theorists.

### Classic Theories of Child Development

http://childstudy.net/cdw.html

### Narrative Psychology Internet and Resource Guide

http://web.lemoyne.edu/~hevern/narpsych.html

### Counselor Net—SUNY Plattsburgh

http://www.plattsburgh.edu/cnet

### The Counseling Web: Counseling Psychology Programs and Resources

http://seamonkey.ed.asu.edu/~gail/resource.htm

### The Counselor Link

http://www.counselorlink.com

### Psych Site

http://kenstange.com/psycsite

This Web site provides psychological resources.

### Psych Web for Psychology Links

http://www.psychwww.com

### Health Resources on the Net

http://www.cc.emory.edu/WHSCL/online.htm

### Counseling Licensing Exam Prep Materials

http://www.a-zuc.com/counseling

### Behavior OnLine: The Mental Health and Behavioral Science Meeting Place

http://www.behavior.net

### Depression Central

`http://www.psycom.net`

### National Depressive and Manic Depressive Association

`http://www.ndmda.org`

This site contains information and advocacy with links to support groups, patient/consumer reports, depression information, patient assistance programs, education, and diagnosis.

### Mental Health Infosource

`http://www.mhsource.com`

### Internet Mental Health Resources

`http://freenet.msp.mn.us/cgi-bin/webglimpse/home/`
`www/root/wgsearch?query=mental+health`

### Your Health Daily

`http://yourhealthdaily.com`

This site offers the latest news and information on mental health from *New York Times* news syndicate.

### Working with Addictive Disorders

`http://www.lasalle.edu/~chapman`

### Internet Mental Health

`http://www.mentalhealth.com`

This site is an online resource for schizophrenia and other mental health information.

### National Council for Community Behavioral Healthcare

`http://www.nccbh.org`

This site contains membership information, educational resources, a marketplace, a job bank, and public policy.

*Research Navigator Guide: Helping Professions*

### Medical and Clinical Supersites for Professionals

`http://members.aol.com/texaspam/admin6.htm`

Pam Pohly's Net Guide contains medical and clinical supersites. A splash page with over fifty sites includes "This Week's Hot Jobs."

### American Managed Behavioral Healthcare Association

`http://www.ambha.org`

These online resources contain membership, links to mental health sites, and reports and studies.

### Trauma and CISD Menu Page

`http://www.eap.com.au/cisd.html`

This site is an employee assistance program for IPS located in Australia.

### At Health Mental Health

`http://www.athealth.com`

This Web site contains a directory of professionals, newsletters, professional registration, treatment centers, a resource link, books for professionals and a psychotropic resource link.

### NAMI

`http://www.nami.org`

National Alliance for the Mentally Ill produces this site, which contains the following links: book reviews, family support, a helpline, and legal issues for the mentally ill.

### Kübler-Ross: Death and Dying

`http://www.elisabethkublerross.com`

### Resources on Death and Dying

`http://www.adec.org/`
`http://www.adec.org/pubs/lmd/lmdltr.htm`

### Bereavement CD

```
http://www.bouldenpublishing.com
Email: jboulden@bouldenpub.com
```

Publications for Children in Distress has an interactive CD for their book, *Saying Good-bye,* which is used by seventy-five percent of the hospices and twenty-five percent of the elementary schools in the United States. The CD-ROM contains the story line of the book with animation, music, and color plus exercises for processing emotions and built-in counselor support for questions children often ask about death. Available from: Dr. Jim Boulden, Publications for Children in Distress, P.O. Box 1186, Westerville, CA 96093, (916) 623-5399 FAX (916) 623-5525

### Florida Mental Health Institute

```
http://hal.fmhi.usf.edu
```

### Dr. Bob's Mental Health Links

```
http://www.dr-bob.org/mental.html
```

### Medweb

```
http://www.cc.emory.edu/WHSCL
```

### 1-800-THERAPIST NETWORK

```
http://www.1-800-therapist.com
```

Kevin Grold, Ph.D. President, 1-800-THERAPIST NETWORK, the largest multidisciplinary therapist referral service. Either fax (619-481-5143), phone (619-481-1515), or Email: referral@1-800-therapist.com

### Deafness

```
http://deafness.about.com
```

### CyberPsychLink

```
http://www.cyber-psych.com/
```

This site includes links and information for Psychology and Behavioral Medicine. Catalogues include listservs, newsgroups, databases, libraries, and software.

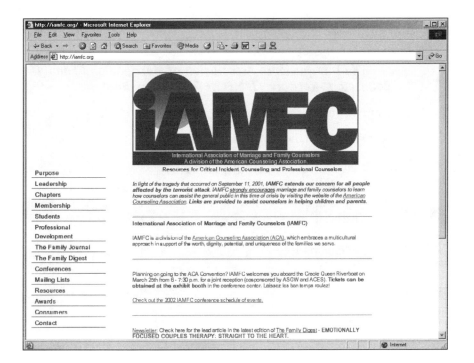

## MARRIAGE AND FAMILY SITES

### *Marriage and Family Web Site*

http://iamfc.org
http://iamfc.org/links.htm

### *KidsPsych*

http://www.kidspsych.org

Developed by the American Psychological Association (APA), KidsPsych is a new "online adventure" for children and their parents. The Shockwave-powered site contains interactive games for children ages one through nine.

### *Family Involvement*

http://pfie.ed.gov

The new Partnerships for Family Involvement in Education (PFIE) home page, developed with *USA Today,* offers a weekly "Spotlight" on education and PFIE issues; examples of how families, schools, businesses, and community and religious organizations are improving education in their communities; and how you can get involved. A "Partner Listing" database can help you find a particular organization among the more than 4,000 PFIE member organizations nationwide.

### The International Association of Marriage and Family Counselors' Network (IAMFCNET-L) Discussion List

```
http://www.iamfc.org
```

Membership in the International Association of Marriage and Family Counselors (IAMFC) is not required to be a part of the listserv, but it is encouraged. To subscribe to the IAMFCNET-L, address an email message to Listserv@listserv.kent.edu and leave the "subject" blank. The text of the message: sub iamfcnet-l <firstname lastname>. For example: sub iamfcnet-l richard watts. Send message

### Sex Surrogates

```
http://iamfc.org/links.htm
```

### Divorce Sites

```
http://www.divorcenet.com/
http://mentalhelp.net/psyhelp/chap10/chap10o.htm
http://www.realtime.net/~mmjw/jw.htm
http://www.divorceinfo.com
```

## CURRENT TRENDS

### Bazelon Center for Mental Health Law

```
http://www.bazelon.org
```

Based in Washington D.C., the Bazelon Center for Mental Health Law is a nonprofit legal advocacy organization for people with mental illness and mental retardation.

### PsychNews Int'l

```
Email: Psychnews@psychologie.de
Email: Pni@badlands.nodak.edu
```

This site describes mental health related resources currently available, or announced, on the Internet. Submit all contributions or corrections for the Resource Update section to the PsychNews Int'l mailboxes.

### Knowledge Exchange Network (KEN)

```
http://www.mentalhealth.org
```

KEN is a one-stop source of information and resources on prevention, treatment, and rehabilitation services for mental illness. KEN is a service of the Center for Mental Health Services, Substance Abuse and Mental Health Services Administration, U.S. Department of Health and Human Services. KEN offers information related to Consumers/Survivors, Managed Care, Children's Mental Health, Statistics, and upcoming conferences and events. KEN offers an online database lookup of mental health resources around the country and in your community. KEN offers an extensive catalog of free publications, many of which can be viewed at the site or downloaded via FTP. All of the publications can be ordered via an online order form.

### Childhood Sexual Abuse Manual

Email: sampson1@ix.netcom.com

The New York State Office of Mental Health is making available a manual to persons working with survivors of childhood sexual abuse. The manual is entitled *Understanding and Dealing with Sexual Abuse Trauma: An Educational Group for Women* and was written by Dr. Kristina Muenzenmaier, Donald Sampson, and others.

### Shamanic Healing for Abuse Survivors

http://www.kitcarson.net/shaman

Shamanic healing Web site for "body, mind, and spirit" specializing in survivors of childhood abuse. This site contains links to relevant sites.

### Sandplay Therapists of America

http://www.sandplayusa.org

### Play Therapy

http://www.amazon.com

Windows to Our Children is a wonderful resource for working with children. Violet Oaklander's model, however, is Gestalt Therapy and if you are looking specifically for ways to use Play Therapy with children, the following books are a great starting point for a non-directive approach:

- *Play Therapy,* Virginia Axline.
- *Play Therapy, The Art of Relationship,* Garry L. Landreth.
- **http://www.amazon.com** and type in Play Therapy.

### Alzheimer Treatment and Cause

http://www.alz.org

### Psychologists' Desk Reference

http://www.oup-usa.org/isbn/0195111869.html

### Self Improvement Online

http://selfgrowth.com/therapy.html

This site contains sponsor Web sites and ninety-four additional related Web sites related to therapy and counseling.

## JOURNALS

### Psychwatch.com Counseling Journals

http://www.psychwatch.com/counsel_journals.htm

This meta-site links to forty counseling journals.

## PSYCHOLOGY JOURNALS

### American Psychiatric Association and American Psychological Association Online Journal

http://www.journals.apa.org/prevention/

A new online journal that is being jointly sponsored by the American Psychiatric Association and the American Psychological Association, by Martin E. P. Seligman and Donald F. Klein. It's also free and contains an email discussion list for subscribers to discuss the latest in psychological and psychiatric outcome/treatment research. Included is information on the Planetree model of patient-centered health care that is emerging as an alternative to traditional managed care. Interestingly, Planetree has not yet filtered down to mental health and counseling but is now represented by fifteen hospitals in the United States, as well as in Norway and England.

### Psycoloquy

http://www.princeton.edu/~harnad/psyc.html

### Theory and Psychology Journal

http://www.psych.ucalgary.ca/thpsyc/

### *Journal of Cognitive Rehabilitation*

`http://www.neuroscience.cntr.com/JCR/NSP/default.htm`

### *Pre- and Perinatal Psychology Journal*

`http://www.birthpsychology.com/journal/index.html`

### *The Sport Psychologist*

`http://www.humankinetics.com/`

### *Behavioral Healthcare & Informatics Tomorrow*

`http://www.bhtomorrow.com`

### *Bulletin of the Menninger Clinic*

`http://www.guilford.com/periodicals/jnme.htm`

### *Journal of Applied Psychology*

`http://www.apa.org/journals/apl.html`

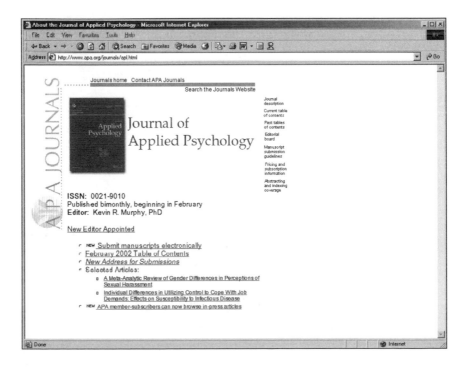

### Journal of Psychology and Human Sexuality

http://www.haworthpressinc.com

### Journal of Social and Clinical Psychology

http://www.guilford.com/periodicals/jnsc.htm

### Genetic, Social, and General Psychology Monographs

http://www.heldref.org/html/body_mono.html

### International Bulletin of Political Psychology

http://www.pr.erau.edu/~security/index.html

### Journal of Applied Behavioral Research

http://www.bellpub.com/jabr

### Journal of Applied Social Psychology

http://www.bellpub.com/jasp

### Journal of Comparative Psychology

http://www.apa.org/journals/com.html

### Journal of Gerontology: Psychological Sciences

http://www.geron.org/journals/psychological.html

### American Psychologist

http://www.apa.org/journals/amp.html

### ReVision: A Journal of Consciousness and Transformation

http://www.heldref.org/html/body_rev.html

### Journal of Humanistic Psychology

http://ahpweb.org/pub/journal/menu.html

### Cultural Diversity and Ethnic Minority Psychology

`http://www.apa.org/journals/cdp.html`

### Journal for Specialists in Group Work

`http://asgw.educ.kent.edu/jsgw`

### Journal of Mind and Behavior

`http://www.ume.maine.edu/~jmb/welcome.html`

### American Journal of Community Psychology

`http://www.kluweronline.com/issn/0091-0562`

### APA Monitor

`http://www.apa.org/monitor`

### Development and Psychopathology

`http://www.journals.cup.org/bin/bladerunner/`
`?30REQEVENT=&REQAUTH=0&116000REQSUB==&REQSTR1=DPP`

### Developmental Review

`http://www.academicpress.com/dr`

### Child and Family Behavior Therapy

`http://web.spectra.net/cgi-bin/haworth/`
`j-title_search?SearchTitle=`

### Child Abuse and Neglect

`http://www.elsevier.nl/locate/chiabuneg`

### Journal of Divorce and Remarriage

`http://www.haworthpressinc.com`

### Counseling and Values

http://www.counseling.org/journals/

### CTOnline

http://www.counseling.org/ctonline

### Prevention and Treatment

http://journals.apa.org/prevention

### ACAeNews

Email: enews@COUNSELING.ORG

### Journal of Redecision Therapy

http://www.themetro.com/redecision

## SOCIAL PSYCHOLOGY JOURNALS

### Journal of Applied Social Psychology

http://www.bellpub.com/jasp

### American Journal of Sociology

http://www.journals.uchicago.edu/AJS/home.html

### Social Psychology Quarterly

http://www.u.arizona.edu/~spq

### European Journal of Social Psychology

http://www.interscience.wiley.com/jpages/0046-2772

### Journal of Personality and Social Psychology

http://www.apa.org/journals/psp.html

### Current Research in Social Psychology

http://www.uiowa.edu/~grpproc/crisp/crisp.html

### Asian Journal of Social Psychology

http://www.blackwellpublishers.co.uk/asp/
journal.asp?ref=13672223

### Sociological Abstracts

http://www.socabs.org

### Transactional Analysis Journal

http://www.tajnet.org

### Ethnic and Racial Studies

http://www.tandf.co.uk/journals/routledge/
01419870.html

### Social Development

http://www.blackwellpublishers.co.uk/asp/
journal.asp?ref=0961205X

### Social Cognition

http://www.guilford.com/periodicals/jnco.htm

### Canadian Journal of Community Mental Health Review

http://info.wlu.ca/~wwwpress/jrls/cjcmh.htm

### Crisis (Journal of Crisis Intervention and Suicide Prevention)

http://www.hhpub.com/journals/crisis/index.html

### Journal of Psychoeducational Assessment (JPA)

http://www.psychoeducational.com

*Research Navigator Guide: Helping Professions*

### Evidenced-Based Mental Health

http://www.ebmentalhealth.com

### Aging and Mental Health

http://www.tandf.co.uk/journals/carfax/13607863.html

### American Indian and Alaska Native Mental Health Research

http://www.uchsc.edu/ai/ncaianmhr/journal/index.htm

### Counseling and Values

http://www.counseling.org/journals/

### Journal of Mental Health

http://www.journals.tandf.co.uk/carfax/09638237.html

# Internet Sites Useful in Social Work

## The Social Work Mega-Sites

### Association of Baccalaureate Social Work Program Directors

http://www.bpdonline.org/

This Web site, which serves as a home page for the BSW program directors, offers a variety of links to a wide range of social work Internet resources.

### Columbia University Social Work Library

http://www.columbia.edu/cu/lweb/indiv/socwk/

Provides links to social work subject guides and Internet resources, social work related electronic journals on the Internet, and current social work monographs from Columbia University.

### The Complete Social Worker Guide to Using the Internet in Social Work

http://www.geocities.com/Heartland/4862/cswhome.html

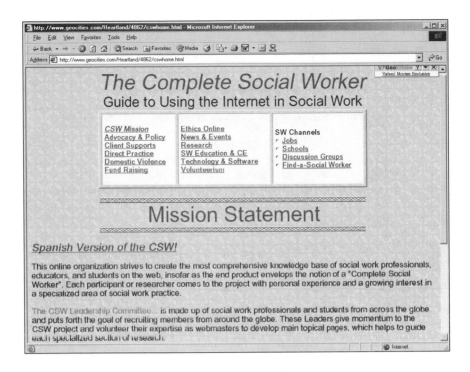

This online organization strives to create the most comprehensive knowledge base of social work professionals, educators, and students on the Web. They provide an impressive set of links to social work resources in a wide range of practice areas.

### Computer Use in Social Services Network (CUSSN)

`http://www2.uta.edu/cussn/`

CUSSNet began in 1985 as a group of FIDONET bulletin boards. Possibly the first social work presence on the Internet, no set of links would be complete without including reference to this site. The site provides links to resources related to computer use in human services, and serves as an important linkage for social workers on the Internet.

### Social Work Gateway

`http://www.chst.soton.ac.uk/webconn.htm`

This site is sponsored by the Computers in Teaching Initiative Centre for Human Services at the University of Southampton (UK). The site provides links in the areas of children and families, community work, social work databases, drugs, eldercare, equal opportunities, human rights, mental health, networks, psychosocial palliative care, social work organizations, social work practice, social work research, social work education, welfare benefits, and more.

### Grassroots Social Science Web Directory

http://www.andrews.edu/SOWK/grassroots.htm

Sponsored by the Social Work Department of Andrews University, this site offers keyword search capabilities and site reviews. The site also offers links to social work content areas, cross-curriculum issues, and other topics, such as social work education, professional organizations, spirituality and alternative therapies, social work technology, and social work journals and e-zines.

### INC: Information For and About Nonprofit Organizations

http://www.nonprofits.org/

The Internet Nonprofit Center is a project of The Evergreen State Society of Seattle, Washington. It offers information for and about nonprofit organizations in the United States, and is the home of the Nonprofit FAQ, the Nonprofit Locator, and the Form 990 Project.

### Shirley's Social Work Web Resources

http://kml.uindy.edu/resources/socialwork/

An impressive list of social work related links from the University of Indianapolis. The Webmistress, Shirley Bigna, advises that her list is selective and limited to those sites which library staff, faculty or students have actually reached. Inclusion of a site indicates that the site was visited and found to have useful information. These links are checked on a rotating basis to verify that they are still active.

### Social Work Access Network

http://www.sc.edu/swan/

SWAN, sponsored by the University of South Carolina College of Social Work, offers one of the most complete listing of Internet resources available for social workers. SWAN organizes links in topical areas such as national organizations, global organizations, US governments, schools of social work, conferences and meeting, and topics by subject. SWAN also has listserv and newsgroup directories.

### Social Work and Social Services Web Sites

http://gwbweb.wustl.edu/websites.html

Hosted by the George Warren Brown School of Social Work, this site offers a tremendous number of links in a wide range of social work practice areas.

### The Social Work Café

`http://www.geocities.com/Heartland/4862/swcafe.html`

This site represents a wealth of resources in a variety of areas for social workers. Hosted as a free service of GeoCities.Com, the Social Work Café is a community of global Social Work professionals, educators, and students who believe in the cross-global exchange of information.

### Social Work Search .com

`http://www.socialworksearch.com/`

This site started in early 1996 as Tom Cleereman's Social Work Site. In April, 2001 Linkpopularity.com reported that over 900 different Web sites on the Internet provide links to socialworksearch.com. Now this former tiny personal Web site became a major portal for the online Social Work community in providing Internet related services to social workers and other helping professionals. Socialworksearch.com has now grown to more than 500 different web pages of services and Internet links, offering the largest online database of services devoted solely to the Social Work profession.

### World Wide Web Resources for Social Workers

`http://www.nyu.edu/socialwork/wwwrsw/`

W3RSW, produced by Gary Holden at NYU, is an amazing resource with nearly 55,000 links to social work resources in a wide range of topics. This site was selected for the *Chronicle of Higher Education's Information Technology Resources* and for the *UniGuide Academic Guide to the Internet* (formerly the National Science Foundation funded *InterNIC Academic Guide to the Internet*).

## Academic Sites

### Columbia University (New York)

`http://www.cc.columbia.edu/cu/ssw/`

A particularly well-designed site, Columbia provides a variety of links to library, computing, and Internet resources for social work.

### Colorado State University

`http://www.cahs.colostate.edu/sw/`

Colorado State provides a nice set of links to other Web resources.

### Grant MacEwan Community College (Alberta, Canada)

`http://www.hcs.gmcc.ab.ca/socialwork`

Great list of international social work resources, with a focus on Canada.

### Jane Addams College of Social Work (Illinois)

`http://www.uic.edu/jaddams/college/`

This site includes information about Hull House Museum, which commemorates the work of social welfare pioneer and peace advocate Jane Addams, her innovative settlement house associates, and the neighborhood they served.

### Ohio State University

`http://www.csw.ohio-state.edu/`

This site features information about two journals sponsored by Ohio State College of Social Work, *Journal of Poverty* and *Journal of Social Work Research and Evaluation.*

### New Mexico State University

`http://www.nmsu.edu/~socwork/`

Provides information about the Family Preservation Institute and other social work related links.

### Rochester Institute of Technology (New York)

`http://www.isc.rit.edu/~694www/`

This is a nicely designed site that offers resources related to social work and deafness and to social work and information technology.

### State University of New York at Albany

`http://www.albany.edu/ssw/`

Offers information about the research activities of the School of Social Welfare.

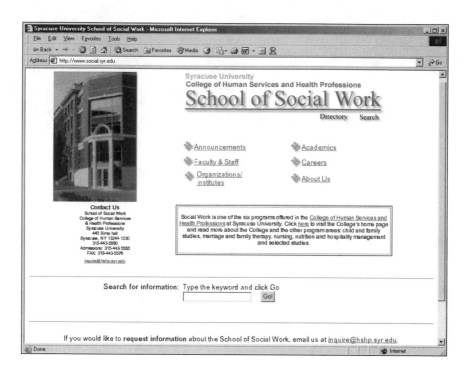

### Syracuse University (New York)

http://www.social.syr.edu/

Offers a comprehensive list of social work links in a wide variety of practice areas.

### Temple University (Pennsylvania)

http://www.temple.edu/socialwork/

Offers some useful Internet resources for social workers.

### University of Bristol (UK)

http://www.bris.ac.uk/Depts/SPS/

The School for Policy Studies is the home of the Policy Press, and offers other social work links related to social policy in the United Kingdom.

### University of Calgary (Alberta, Canada)

http://fsw.ucalgary.ca/

Easy-to-use site offers resources that are useful to students, faculty and staff at the Faculty of Social Work and others in the social work field.

### University of California at Berkeley

http://socialwelfare.berkeley.edu/

Berkeley offers a variety of links to social work resources on the Net.

### University of Central Lancashire (UK)

http://www.uclan.ac.uk/facs/health/socwork/
socihom1.htm

Provides access to lots of social work sites including *The Social Work Student,* Britain's first online, student refereed journal and *Social Work Research,* a non-critical listing of research reports and academic papers relating to social work.

### University of Chicago (Illinois)

http://www.ssa.uchicago.edu/

This site offers the *Advocate's Forum,* a social work journal managed entirely by social work students.

### University of East Anglia, Norwich (UK)

http://www.uea.ac.uk/menu/acad_depts/swk/

Provides information about the Centre for Research on the Child and Family and the Family Support Network.

### University of Kansas

http://www.socwel.ukans.edu/

Provides a bibliography for the strengths perspective in social work, social science resources, information from Office of Social Policy Analysis and the Kansas Kids Count home page.

### University of Michigan

http://www.ssw.umich.edu/

Offers important resources for social work students and information about ongoing research at the University of Michigan.

### University of Oxford (UK)

http://marx.apsoc.ox.ac.uk/

Provides information about current research at the University of Oxford, recent publications, and useful links.

### University of Pennsylvania

http://www.ssw.upenn.edu/

The University of Pennsylvania site provides information about current research efforts of the School of Social Work.

### University of South Carolina

http://www.sc.edu/cosw/

The University of South Carolina is the home of the Social Work Access Network (SWAN) and sponsors an annual national Technology Conference for social work.

### University of South Florida

http://www.cas.usf.edu/social_work/

Provides a variety of resources for social work students that are useful for seasoned practitioners as well.

### University of Southern California

http://www.usc.edu/dept/socialwork/

USC offers the Social Science and Humanities Center Social Work Collection, which provides a wealth of links for social work scholars.

### University of Tennessee–Knoxville

http://www.csw.utk.edu/

Provides a social work discussion area, information about the Children's Mental Health Services Research Area, and links to other important resources.

### University of Texas at Arlington

http://www2.uta.edu/ssw/

The home of CUSSNET (Computer Users in Human Services), UTA offers a variety of informational links for students and practitioners.

### University of Texas at Austin

http://www.utexas.edu/depts/sswork/

Provides a listing of the activities of their Center for Social Work Research.

### University of Utah

http://www.socwk.utah.edu/

The home base of the author, the site provides information about ongoing research projects and related resources, as well as information about the new Technology-Enhanced Doctoral program.

### University of Washington

http://depts.washington.edu/sswweb/

In addition to the usual links, UW offers *Policy Watch,* a more-or-less weekly bulletin about issues and events in Olympia during the legislative session, focused primarily on social welfare, low-income, and related health concerns before the legislature.

### University of Wisconsin–Madison

http://polyglot.lss.wisc.edu/socwork/

Offers information about The Institute for Research on Poverty, The La-Follette Institute of Public Policy, and the UW Homelessness Project.

### University of York (UK)

http://www.york.ac.uk/depts/spsw/

This UK site offers a useful Social Policy Resource Guide.

### Washington University: George Warren Brown School of Social Work (Missouri)

http://gwbweb.wustl.edu/

One of the most comprehensive sites in social work education, these pages offer information about research projects at GWB and a complete list of informational links in a variety of practice areas. The Social Work and Social Services Jobs Database is a valuable resource for all social workers.

## Government Resources

### Administration for Children and Families

http://www.acf.dhhs.gov/

The Administration on Children, Youth and Families (ACYF) administers the major Federal programs that support: social services that promote the positive growth and development of children and youth and their families; protective services and shelter for children and youth in at-risk situations; child care for working families and families on public assistance; and adoption for children with special needs.

### Bureau of the Census

http://www.census.gov/

The Census Bureau Web site is designed to enable intuitive use of their Internet offerings, so users need not to be familiar with the Census Bureau's internal organizational structure to effectively locate and use the resources the site has to offer.

### Bureau of Justice Statistics

http://www.ojp.usdoj.gov/bjs/

BJS collects, analyzes, publishes, and disseminates information on crime, criminal offenders, victims of crime, and the operation of justice systems at all levels of government.

### Bureau of Labor Statistics

http://stats.bls.gov/

The Bureau of Labor Statistics (BLS) is the principal fact-finding agency for the Federal Government in the broad field of labor economics and statistics. The BLS is an independent national statistical agency that collects, processes, analyzes, and disseminates essential statistical data to the American public, the U.S. Congress, other Federal agencies, State and local governments, business, and labor. The BLS also serves as a statistical resource to the Department of Labor.

### Canadian Government Main Site

http://canada.gc.ca/

The Government of Canada Site is the Internet electronic access point through which Internet users around the world can obtain information about Canada, its government and its services. Direct links are also provided from this site to government departments and agencies that have Internet facilities.

### Catalog of Federal Domestic Assistance

http://aspe.os.dhhs.gov/cfda/

The Catalog of Federal Domestic Assistance Programs (CFDA) is a government-wide compendium of all 1,381 Federal programs, projects, services, and activities that provide assistance or benefits to the American public. These programs provide grants, loans, loan guarantees, services, information, scholarships, training, insurance, etc.

### Centers for Disease Control

http://www.cdc.gov/

The Centers for Disease Control and Prevention (CDC), located in Atlanta, Georgia, USA, is an agency of the Department of Health and Human Services. Its mission is to promote health and quality of life by preventing and controlling disease, injury, and disability. The site provides health news, publications, software, data and statistics, and information about funding and programs.

### Center for Substance Abuse Prevention

http://www.samhsa.gov/centers/csap/csap.html

CSAP's mission is to provide national leadership in the Federal effort to prevent alcohol, tobacco, and illicit drug problems. CSAP fosters the development of comprehensive, culturally appropriate prevention policies and systems that are based on scientifically defensible principles and target both individuals and the environments in which they live.

Research Navigator Guide: Helping Professions

### Center for Substance Abuse Treatment

`http://www.samhsa.gov/centers/csat/csat.html`

The Center for Substance Abuse Treatment (CSAT) was created in October 1992 with the Congressional mandate to expand the availability of effective treatment and recovery services for alcohol and drug problems. CSAT works cooperatively across the private and public treatment spectrum to identify, develop, and support policies, approaches, and programs that enhance and expand treatment services for individuals who abuse alcohol and other drugs and that address individuals' addiction-related problems.

### Child Support Enforcement

`http://www.acf.dhhs.gov/programs/cse/`

Child Support Enforcement helps States locate absent parents, establish paternity, and enforce legal orders for support.

### Corporation for National and Community Service

`http://www.cns.gov/`

This site provides information about volunteer opportunities, including VISTA, AmeriCorps, Senior Corps, Learn and Serve America, and National Service Scholarships.

### Department of Health and Human Services (DHHS)

http://www.os.dhhs.gov/

The Department of Health and Human Services is the United States government's principal agency for protecting the health of all Americans and providing essential human services, especially for those who are least able to help themselves. It is the largest grant-making agency in the federal government, providing some 60,000 grants per year. HHS' Medicare program is the nation's largest health insurer, handling more than 800 million claims per year.

### Federal Emergency Management Agency

http://www.fema.gov/

The Federal Emergency Management Agency (FEMA) is an independent agency of the federal government, reporting to the President. Founded in 1979, FEMA's mission is to reduce loss of life and property and protect our nation's critical infrastructure from all types of hazards through a comprehensive, risk-based, emergency management program of mitigation, preparedness, response and recovery.

### FedWorld Information Network Home Page

http://www.fedworld.gov/

Access to thousands of U.S. Government Web sites, more than 500,000 U.S. government documents, databases, and other information products.

### Government Information Sharing Project

http://govinfo.kerr.orst.edu/

The Government Information Sharing Project was initiated with funding from the U.S. Department of Education and is administered at Oregon State University Libraries. The original goal of the project was to demonstrate improved access to electronic government information, especially for remote users (such as rural Oregon residents) and the general public. Beginning in 1995, the Project developed World Wide Web access to a variety of federal statistical information issued on CD-ROM and distributed through the Federal Depository Library Program. Through the Web, the audience of the site has quickly become a national and international one, including libraries, community developers, small and large businesses, researchers, students, journalists, agencies, and many more.

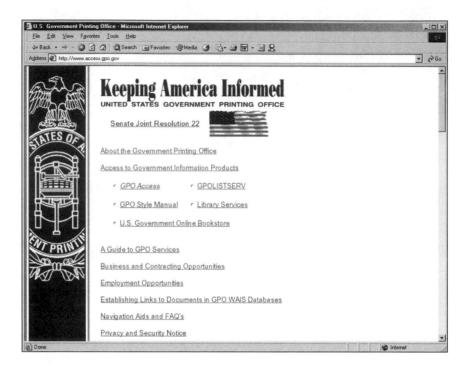

### Government Printing Office

`http://www.access.gpo.gov/`

The Government Printing Office (GPO) prints, binds, and distributes the publications of the Congress as well as the executive departments and establishments of the Federal Government. Distribution is being accomplished on an increasing basis via various electronic media in accordance with Public Law 103-40, "The Government Printing Office Electronic Information Access Enhancement Act of 1993."

### Centers for Medicare & Medicaid Services (CMS)

`http://www.cms.gov`

The Centers for Medicare & Medicaid Services (formerly the Health Care Financing Administration) provides health insurance for over 74 million Americans through Medicare, Medicaid and State Children's Health Insurance Program (SCHIP). In addition to providing health insurance, CMS also performs a number of quality-focused activities, including regulation of laboratory testing (CLIA), development of coverage policies, and quality-of-care improvement. CMA maintains oversight of the survey and certification of nursing homes and continuing care), and makes available to beneficiaries, providers, researchers and State surveyors information about these activities and nursing home quality.

## Healthfinder®

`http://www.healthfinder.gov/`

Healthfinder® is a gateway consumer health and human services information Web site from the United States government. Healthfinder® can lead you to selected online publications, clearinghouses, databases, Web sites, and support and self-help groups, as well as the government agencies and not-for-profit organizations that produce reliable information for the public. Launched in April 1997, Healthfinder® served Internet users over 1.7 million times in its first year online.

### Health Resources and Services Administration

`http://www.hrsa.dhhs.gov/`

The Health Resources and Services Administration (HRSA) directs national health programs which improve the health of the Nation by assuring quality health care to underserved, vulnerable and special-need populations and by promoting appropriate health professions workforce capacity and practice, particularly in primary care and public health.

### Hispanic Agenda for Action

`http://www.omhrc.gov/haa/`

Hispanics are the fastest growing minority population in the U.S. and are predicted to be the largest minority group in the next 15 years. The adverse social conditions suffered by many Hispanics are severely challenging those institutions and service structures, which struggle to provide and deliver quality services to Hispanic families and communities. HHS is determined to work more closely with its partner institutions and organizations that serve the Hispanic community to better address the needs of the growing Hispanic population, together with other customer groups. As one of many efforts to meet this objective, they have established the Hispanic Agenda for Action (HAA) Home Page to serve as a Departmental Internet link for improving service delivery. The HAA Home Page features services provided by the Department that are of particular interest to the Hispanic community and organizations serving Hispanics. Links to services outside the Department also are featured.

### House of Representatives

`http://www.house.gov/`

Contact your congressional representative the easy way.

### Indian Health Service

`http://www.ihs.gov/`

The Indian Health Service (IHS), an agency within the Department of Health and Human Services, is responsible for providing federal health services to American Indians and Alaska Natives. The provision of health services to members of federally-recognized tribes grew out of the special government-to-government relationship between the federal government and Indian tribes.

### Library of Congress

`http://lcweb.loc.gov/`

The Library of Congress mission is to make its resources available and useful to the Congress and the American people and to sustain and preserve a universal collection of knowledge and creativity for future generations. This World Wide Web site allows the Library of Congress to historical collections, their catalog, the text and images from major exhibitions, the THOMAS database of current and historical information on the U.S. Congress, a Learning Page for K–12 students and teachers, and much more.

### Maternal and Child Health Bureau

`http://www.mchb.hrsa.gov/`

The Maternal and Child Health Bureau (MCHB) is charged with the primary responsibility for promoting and improving the health of our Nation's mothers and children. It predecessor, the Children's Bureau, was established in 1912. In 1935, Congress enacted Title V of the Social Security Act, which authorized the Maternal and Child Health Services Programs—providing a foundation and structure for assuring the health of mothers and children now for more than 60 years. Today, Title V is administered by the Maternal and Child Health Bureau as part of the Health Resources and Services Administration, Public Health Service, U.S. Department of Health and Human Services.

### National Association of State Information Resource Executive's StateSearch

`https://www.nascio.org/statesearch/`

StateSearch is a service of the National Association of State Information Resource Executives and is designed to serve as a topical clearinghouse to state government information on the Internet.

### National Cancer Institute

http://www.nci.nih.gov/

The National Cancer Institute (NCI) is a component of the National Institutes of Health (NIH), one of eight agencies that compose the Public Health Service (PHS) in the Department of Health and Human Services (DHHS). The NCI, established under the National Cancer Act of 1937, is the Federal Government's principal agency for cancer research and training. The National Cancer Act of 1971 broadened the scope and responsibilities of the NCI and created the National Cancer Program. Over the years, legislative amendments have maintained the NCI authorities and responsibilities and added new information dissemination mandates as well as a requirement to assess the incorporation of state-of-the-art cancer treatments into clinical practice.

### The National Criminal Justice Reference Service

http://www.ncjrs.org/

The National Criminal Justice Reference Service (NCJRS) is one of the most extensive sources of information on criminal and juvenile justice in the world, providing services to an international community of policymakers and professionals. NCJRS is a collection of clearinghouses supporting all bureaus of the U.S. Department of Justice, Office of Justice Programs: the National Institute of Justice, the Office of Juvenile Justice and Delinquency Prevention, the Bureau of Justice Statistics, the Bureau of Justice Assistance, the Office for Victims of Crime, and the OJP Program Offices. It also supports the Office of National Drug Control Policy.

### National Institute of Alcohol Abuse and Alcoholism

http://www.niaaa.nih.gov/

In 1970, the United States Congress recognized alcohol abuse and alcoholism as major public health problems and created the National Institute on Alcohol Abuse and Alcoholism (NIAAA) to combat them. The Web site provides information about reports and publications available from the Institute, as well as access to the ETOH database.

### National Institute of Child Health and Human Development

http://www.nichd.nih.gov/

The National Institute of Child Health and Human Development is part of the National Institutes of Health, U.S. Department of Health and Human Services. The NICHD conducts and supports laboratory, clinical and epidemiological research on the reproductive, neurobiological, developmental, and behavioral processes that determine and maintain the health of children, adults, families and populations.

### National Institute of Drug Abuse

`http://www.nida.nih.gov/`

The National Institute on Drug Abuse (NIDA) supports over 85 percent of the world's research on the health aspects of drug abuse and addiction, ranging from the most fundamental and essential questions about drug abuse; the molecule to managed care, and from DNA to community outreach research. The NIDA Web page is an important part of NIDA's effort to ensure the rapid and effective transfer of scientific data to policy makers, drug abuse practitioners, other health care practitioners and the general public.

### National Institutes of Health

`http://www.nih.gov/`

The NIH mission is to uncover new knowledge that will lead to better health for everyone. NIH works toward that mission by: conducting research in its own laboratories; supporting the research of non-Federal scientists in universities, medical schools, hospitals, and research institutions throughout the country and abroad; helping in the training of research investigators; and fostering communication of biomedical information.

### National Institute of Justice

`http://www.ojp.usdoj.gov/nij/`

The National Institute of Justice (NIJ) is the research agency of the U.S. Department of Justice. Created by the Omnibus Crime Control and Safe Streets Act of 1968, as amended, NIJ is authorized to support research, evaluation, and demonstration programs, development of technology, and both national and international information dissemination.

### National Institute of Mental Health

`http://www.nimh.nih.gov/`

NIMH is the foremost mental health research organization in the world, with a mission of improving the treatment, diagnosis, and prevention of mental disorders such as schizophrenia and depressive illnesses, and other conditions that affect millions of Americans, including children and adolescents. The Web site provides information about mental health disorders, news and events, grants and contracts, and NIMH-sponsored research activities.

### National Library of Medicine

http://www.nlm.nih.gov/

The NLM site provides individuals free access to MEDLINE for free. The visible human project and other offerings make this a "must browse" site.

### National Institute on Aging

http://www.nia.nih.gov

The National Institute on Aging (NIA) leads a broad scientific effort to understand the nature of aging and to extend the healthy, active years of life. In 1974, Congress granted authority to form the National Institute on Aging to provide leadership in aging research, training, health information dissemination, and other programs relevant to aging and older people. Subsequent amendments to this legislation designated the NIA as the primary federal agency on Alzheimer's disease research.

### Office of Juvenile Justice and Delinquency Prevention

http://ojjdp.ncjrs.org/

The OJJDP Web site is designed to provide information and resources on both general areas of interest about juvenile justice and delinquency including conferences, funding opportunities, and new publications and the comprehensive strategy as a framework for communities to combat youth crime.

### Office of Population Affairs

http://opa.osophs.dhhs.gov

The Office of Population Affairs provides resources and policy advice on population, family planning, reproductive health, and adolescent pregnancy issues. OPA also administers two grant programs, the national Family Planning Program and the Adolescent Family Life Program.

### PREVLINE: Prevention Online

http://www.health.org/

The National Clearinghouse for Alcohol and Drug Information, NCADI, is the world's largest repository of information on substance abuse prevention and policy. PREVLINE presents information on drug and alcohol abuse, alcoholism prevention, overdoses, addiction, and treatment through links to thousands of documents, searchable databases, statistics, press releases, public domain graphics, and interactive forums.

### Rural Empowerment Zones and Enterprise Communities

http://www.ezec.gov/

The Rural Empowerment Zone/Enterprise Communities Home Page is designed to promote the exchange of information about the Presidential Empowerment Initiative. Here you will find information about the purposes and organization of the Initiative and the Empowerment Zones, Enterprise Communities, and Champion Communities participating in the Initiative. In addition, the REZ/EC Home Page provides a toolbox of information to help communities develop and implement effective strategic plans for community and economic development.

### Rural Housing Service

http://www.rurdev.usda.gov/rhs/

The USDA Rural Housing Service has various programs available to aid in the development of rural America. Rural Housing programs are divided into three categories: Community Facilities (CF), Single Family Housing (SFH), and Multi-Family Housing (MFH). These programs were formerly operated by the Rural Development Administration and the Farmers Home Administration.

### Senate Home Page

http://www.senate.gov/

Contact your Senators the easy way.

### Social Security Administration

http://www.ssa.gov/

Social Security Online provides a wealth of information about the Social Security Administration, enabling users to better negotiate the maze of services available.

### Substance Abuse and Mental Health Services Administration

http://www.samhsa.gov/

SAMHSA's mission is to assure that quality substance abuse and mental health services are available to the people who need them and to ensure that prevention and treatment knowledge is used more effectively in the general health care system.

### Thomas—U.S. Congress on the Internet

`http://thomas.loc.gov/`

Current US Federal Legislative Information, including bills, laws, Congressional Record, reports, and links to further information.

### Veterans Affairs

`http://www.va.gov/`

The Department of Veterans Affairs (VA) Web site provides information on VA programs, veteran's benefits, VA facilities worldwide, and VA medical automation software. The site serves several major constituencies including the veteran and his/her dependents, Veterans Service Organizations, the military, the general public, and VA employees around the world. Documents on the site are linked from their table of contents and searchable by keyword.

### White House

`http://www.whitehouse.gov/`

This site links users to the executive branch of the United States government. The site includes an archive of White House documents.

### YouthInfo

`http://www.acf.dhhs.gov/programs/fysb/youthinfo/`

YouthInfo is a Web site created by the U.S. Department of Health and Human Services (HHS) and currently maintained by the Family and Youth Services Bureau (FYSB) within HHS. The HHS and FYSB designed this site for those interested in learning about America's young people, their development into productive adults and engaged citizens, and ways to help them achieve their full potential. YouthInfo currently includes the following: a statistical profile of America's teenagers; the latest reports and publications about adolescents; information for parents of teens; speeches by federal officials on youth topics; links to youth-related Web sites at HHS, other federal agencies and private foundations and research organizations.

## Professional Association Sites

### Alliance for Psychosocial Nursing

`http://www.psychnurse.org/`

The APN is the primary organization for psychiatric and mental health nurses worldwide. The site serves as a resource and lobbying force for nurses and their patients and contains information about memberships and meetings, a job bank, online journal, and discussion areas.

### American Association of Community Psychiatrists

`http://www.comm.psych.pitt.edu/`

The AACP seeks to promote and maintain excellence in the care of patients through the organization of psychiatrists practicing community mental health on state, regional and national levels.

### American Association for Marriage and Family Therapy

`http://www.aamft.org/`

The American Association for Marriage and Family Therapy (AAMFT) is the professional association for the field of marriage and family therapy. We represent the professional interests of more than 23,000 marriage and family therapists throughout the United States, Canada and abroad.

### American Association of Pastoral Counselors

`http://www.aapc.org/`

Pastoral Counseling is a mental health discipline that integrates psychotherapy and spirituality. Pastoral Counselors are mental health professionals who have received specialized graduate training in both religion and the behavioral sciences, and practice the integrated discipline of pastoral counseling. The American Association of Pastoral Counselors (AAPC) represents and sets professional standards for over 3,200 Pastoral Counselors and more than 100 pastoral counseling centers in the United States.

### American Association of Health Plans

`http://www.aahp.org/`

The American Association of Health Plans (AAHP), located in Washington, DC, represents more than 1,000 HMOs, PPOs and other network-based plans. The site offers a wealth of information related to health care and legislative advocacy.

### American Counseling Association

`http://www.counseling.org/`

The American Counseling Association is a not-for-profit, professional and educational organization that is dedicated to the growth and enhancement of the counseling profession.

### American Medical Association

`http://www.ama-assn.org/`

Since its founding in 1847 by a group of physicians concerned about advancing the quality of medical education, science, and practice, the American Medical Association's core purpose has been to promote the art and science of medicine and the betterment of public health.

### American Mental Health Counselors Association

`http://www.amhca.org/`

The mission of the American Mental Health Counselors Association is to enhance the profession of mental health counseling through licensing, advocacy, education, and professional development. Their vision is to be the national organization representing licensed mental health counselors, and state chapters, with consistent standards of education, training, licensing, practice, advocacy, and ethics.

### American Psychiatric Association

`http://www.psych.org/`

The American Psychiatric Association is a medical specialty society recognized worldwide. Its 40,500 U.S. and international physicians specialize in the diagnosis and treatment of mental and emotional illnesses and substance use disorders.

### American Public Health Association

http://www.apha.org/

The American Public Health Association (APHA) is the oldest and largest organization of public health professionals in the world, representing more than 50,000 members from over 50 occupations of public health.

### Association for Behavior Analysis

http://www.wmich.edu/aba/

The Association for Behavior Analysis is dedicated to promoting the experimental, theoretical, and applied analysis of behavior. It encompasses contemporary scientific and social issues, theoretical advances, and the dissemination of professional and public information.

### Association for Community Organization and Social Administration

http://www.acosa.org/

The Association for Community Organization and Social Administration, formed in 1987, is a membership organization for community organizers, planners, activists, administrators, policy practice specialists, students, and professors. ACOSA members represent a variety of disciplines and professional fields that strive to strengthen community organization and social administration in social work practice and education.

### Association for Oncology Social Work

http://www.aosw.org/

A nonprofit, international organization dedicated to the enhancement of psychosocial services to people with cancer and their families. AOSW is dedicated to increasing awareness about the social, emotional, educational, and spiritual needs of cancer patients. It supports its members' commitment to helping and advocating for cancer patients by providing continuing education through conferences and publications; promoting clinical research; and fostering networking to address common issues and concerns.

### Association of Baccalaureate Program Directors

http://www.bpdonline.org/

This professional association represents directors of baccalaureate social work programs accredited through the Council on Social Work Education.

### Association of Social Work Boards

http://www.aswb.org/

The Association of Social Work Boards (ASWB) is the association of boards that regulate social work. Incorporated in 1979 as the American Association of State Social Work Boards, an organization devoted to consumer protection, ASWB membership now includes 49 states, the District of Columbia, the Virgin Islands, and Alberta, Canada.

### Australian Association of Social Work

http://www.aasw.asn.au/

The objectives of the Australian Association of Social Workers Ltd. are to promote the profession of social work, to provide an organization through which social workers can develop a professional identity, to establish, monitor and improve practice standards, to contribute to the development of social work knowledge, to advocate on behalf of clients, and to actively support social structures and policies pursuant to the promotion of social justice.

### British Association of Social Workers

http://www.basw.co.uk/

BASW is the largest organization of professional social workers in the United Kingdom. They speak on all issues that affect the professional standing of social work. Members come from a wide range of agencies in the Local Authority, Voluntary, Independent and Private sectors throughout the United Kingdom. BASW campaigns for improvements to legislation, for social justice and the quality of social work services and good practice.

### Clinical Social Work Federation

http://www.webcom.com/nfscsw/

The Clinical Social Work Federation is a confederation of 31 state societies for clinical social work. Their state societies are formed as voluntary associations for the purpose of promoting the highest standards of professional education and clinical practice. Each society is active with legislative advocacy and lobbying efforts for adequate and appropriate mental health services and coverage at their state and national levels of government.

### Computer Use in Social Services Network

http://www2.uta.edu/cussn/

The Computer Use in Social Services Network (CUSSN) is an informal association of professionals interested in exchanging information and experiences on using computers in the human services. It has been in existence since 1981.

### Council on Social Work Education

http://www.cswe.org/

CSWE is a national association that preserves and enhances the quality of social work education for practice that promotes the goals of individual and community well being and social justice. CSWE pursues this mission through setting and maintaining policy and program standards, accrediting bachelor's and master's degree programs in social work, promoting research and faculty development, and advocating for social work education.

### HUSITA: Human Service Information Technology Applications

http://www.husita.org/

Husita is an international association of information technology (IT) innovators in human services dedicated to promoting the ethical and effective use of IT to better serve humanity. Husita's focus and expertise is situated at the intersection of three core domains: information technology; human services and social development. With an emphasis on human centeredness and social justice, Husita strives to promote international knowledge development, dissemination and transfer of technology within human services. It achieves this through multidisciplinary leadership in international conferences, publications, collaboration and consultation directed particularly at IT applications and innovations that promote social betterment.

### Institute for Mental Health Initiatives

http://www.gwumc.edu/sphhs/imhi/

Institute for Mental Health Initiatives (IMHI), a nonprofit organization of mental health professionals, promotes emotional well being in children, families, and their communities. It makes mental health research accessible to the media and the general public. IMHI builds bridges between clinicians and researchers in the field of mental health, the general public, and the members of the media.

### International Association of Group Psychotherapy

http://www.psych.mcgill.ca/labs/iagp/IAGP.html

The purpose of the IAGP is to serve the development of group psychotherapy, as a field of practice, training, and scientific study, by means of international conferences, publications, and other forms of communication. The assumption is that there is mutual respect between representatives of differing theories and practices concerned with the use and study of group resources in psychotherapy and in dealing with other human problems.

### International Federation of Social Workers

http://www.ifsw.org/

The International Federation of Social Workers is a successor to the International Permanent Secretariat of Social Workers, which was founded in Paris in 1928 and was active until the outbreak of World War II. It was not until 1950, at the time of the International Conference of Social Work in Paris, that the decision was made to create the International Federation of Social Workers, an international organization of professional social workers.

### Irish Association of Social Workers

http://iasw.eire.org/

The Irish Association of Social Workers (IASW) was founded in 1971. It is the national organization of professional social workers in the Republic of Ireland.

### Latino Social Workers Organization

http://www.lswo.org/

The Latino Social Workers Organization provides information resources and networking for Latino social workers and social work students.

### Mental Health in Corrections Consortium

http://www.mhcca.org/

MHCC is dedicated to being a leading voice for mental health providers within the criminal justice system, primarily corrections, and providing the highest quality of training related to mental health issues within criminal justice.

### National Alliance for Hispanic Health

http://www.hispanichealth.org/

The National Alliance for Hispanic Health focuses on the health, mental health, and human services needs of the diverse Hispanic communities. The Alliance's membership consists of thousands of front-line health and human services providers and organizations serving Hispanic communities. The organization was founded in Los Angeles in 1973 as the Coalition of Spanish-Speaking Mental Health Organizations to represent and advocate for the mental health needs of Mexican American, Puerto Rican, Cuban

American, Central American, and South American communities in the United States.

### The National Association of Black Social Workers (NABSW)

`http://www.nabsw.org/`

The National Association of Black Social Workers, Inc. is designed to promote the welfare, survival, and liberation of communities of African ancestry. Members of the NABSW recognize the necessity of Black community control and accountability of self to the Black community.

### National Association of Social Workers (NASW)

`http://www.socialworkers.org/`

NASW is the largest association of professional social workers in the United States. With more than 155,000 members in 56 chapters, NASW promotes, develops and protects the practice of social work and social workers. NASW also seeks to enhance the well being of individuals, families, and communities through its work and through its advocacy.

### National Association of State Mental Health Program Directors

`http://www.nasmhpd.org/`

The National Association of State Mental Health Program Directors (NASMHPD) organizes to reflect and advocate for the collective interests of State Mental Health Authorities and their directors at the national level. NASMHPD analyzes trends in the delivery and financing of mental health services and builds and disseminates knowledge and experience reflecting the integration of public mental health programming in evolving healthcare environments.

### National Council for Community Behavioral Healthcare

`http://www.nccbh.org/`

The National Council for Community Behavioral Healthcare was founded in 1970 to implement a vision and set of beliefs through membership, advocacy and education. Through their work in the public interest, they advocate before the White House, Congress, and federal agencies to advance the interests of our members and the consumers that they serve.

### National Institute for Social Work

`http://www.nisw.org.uk/`

The National Institute for Social Work is the only independent national organization in the United Kingdom specializing exclusively in the personal social services. Founded over 30 years ago, the Institute is at the forefront of social work and social care, actively raising standards and promoting good practice in the public, independent, and voluntary sectors.

### Society for Social Work and Research

http://www.sswr.org/

The Society for Social Work and Research was founded in 1994 as a free-standing organization that works collaboratively with other organizations that are committed to improving the support for research among social workers.

### Society for Social Work Leadership in Healthcare

http://www.sswlhc.org/

The Society for Social Work Leadership in Healthcare is an association dedicated to promoting the universal availability, accessibility, coordination, and effectiveness of health care that addresses the psychosocial components of health and illness.

### World Federation of Mental Health

http://www.wfmh.com/

The World Federation for Mental Health is an international nonprofit advocacy organization founded in 1948 to advance, among all peoples and nations, the prevention of mental and emotional disorders, the proper treatment and care of those with such disorders, and the promotion of mental health. The Federation achieves its goals through public education programs such as World Mental Health Day, research through collaborating centers at major universities, consultation to the United Nations and its specialized agencies, and a regional structure for organizing project work at the community level.

## Electronic Journals and Newsletters

### Action Research International

http://www.scu.edu.au/schools/gcm/ar/ari/arihome.html

*Action Research International* is a refereed on-line journal of action research. Published in Australia, it has an international editorial panel and is sponsored by the Institute of Workplace Research Learning and Development within the Graduate College of Management at Southern Cross University.

### The Advocate's Forum

http://www.ssa.uchicago.edu/publications/
advoforum.shtml

A social work journal managed entirely by University of Chicago students with support from the Office of External Affairs. Inside you will find substantive articles reflecting the diversity of interests, ideas, and concerns of social work students and graduates.

### Age and Ageing

http://ageing.oupjournals.org/

An international journal publishing refereed original articles and commissioned reviews on geriatric medicine and gerontology. Its range includes research on aging and clinical, epidemiological, and psychological aspects of later life.

### AIDS Book Review Journal

http://www.uic.edu/depts/lib/aidsbkrv

An electronic journal reviewing books, videos, journal titles, and other materials covering AIDS, safer sex, sexually transmitted diseases, and other related materials, published irregularly by the University of Illinois at Chicago Library.

### Alcohol Alerts

http://www.niaaa.nih.gov/publications/alalerts.htm

A quarterly bulletin of the National Institute on Alcohol Abuse and Alcoholism that disseminates important research findings on a single aspect of alcohol abuse and alcoholism.

### American Journal on Addictions

http://www.aaap.org/journal/journalindex.html

Contents of issues and abstracts of articles from *AJA*, an authoritative source of new information on drug abuse and the addictions.

### American Medical Association Publishing

http://pubs.ama-assn.org/

Web editions of the AMA's Scientific Publications and *American Medical News* and links to condition-specific Web sites.

### APA Addictions Newsletter

http://www.kumc.edu/addictions_newsletter/

An online publication of The American Psychological Association, Division 50.

### APA Journals

http://www.apa.org/journals/

A listing of all journals published by the American Psychological Association.

### Canadian Journal of Behavioural Science

http://www.cpa.ca/ac-main.html

Abstracts and full-text versions of articles.

### The CATO Journal

http://www.cato.org/pubs/journal/cato_journal.html

Founded in 1977, the Cato Institute is a nonpartisan public policy research foundation headquartered in Washington, D.C. The Cato Institute seeks to broaden the parameters of public policy debate to allow consideration of more options that are consistent with the traditional American principles of limited government, individual liberty, and peace. *The Cato Journal* is an interdisciplinary journal of public policy analysis.

### Child and Adolescent Psychiatry

http://www.priory.co.uk/psychild.htm

Online journal featuring articles relevant to the treatment of children and adolescents.

### Child Maltreatment

http://www.sagepub.co.uk/journals/details/j0119.html

*Child Maltreatment* is the main vehicle of the American Professional Society on the Abuse of Children. Its purpose is to publish longer and more in-depth analyses of theoretical, practice, and policy issues. In addition, CM is an outlet for high-quality original empirical research and reviews of the research literature. It is now available electronically.

### Child Welfare Review

http://www.childwelfare.com/kids/news.htm

Research Navigator Guide: Helping Professions

An electronic journal for coverage of issues related to the well being of children. It contains both links to articles related to child welfare and original articles.

### The Chronicle of Philanthropy

http://philanthropy.com/

*The Chronicle of Philanthropy* is an important news source for charity leaders, fund raisers, grant makers, and other people involved in philanthropic enterprise.

### Current Research in Social Psychology

http://www.uiowa.edu/~grpproc/crisp/crisp.html

A peer reviewed, electronic journal covering all aspects of social psychology sponsored by the Center for the Study of Group Processes at the University of Iowa.

### Electronic Journals and Periodicals in Psychology and Related Fields

http://psych.hanover.edu/Krantz/journal.html

A regularly updated listing of psychology-relevant journals.

### The Future of Children

http://www.futureofchildren.org/

Produced by the Center for the Future of Children, The David and Lucile Packard Foundation, *The Future of Children* is published three times a year and (mostly) reproduced on this site. Links to previous editions are available.

### Harvard Mental Health Letter

http://www.health.harvard.edu/section.cfm?id=17

Selected articles from the paper publication.

### Hunger Notes

http://www.worldhunger.org/

*Hunger Notes* is an online journal that is sponsored by the World Hunger Education Service.

### Journal of Applied Behavior Analysis

http://www.envmed.rochester.edu/wwwrap/behavior/jaba/

Abstracts and tables of contents.

### Journal of Children and Poverty

http://www.tandf.co.uk/journals/carfax/10796126.html

*The Journal of Children and Poverty* is a publication of the Institute for Children and Poverty, the research and training division of Homes for the Homeless. It offers a forum for the presentation of research and policy initiatives in the areas of education, social services, public policy, and welfare reform as they affect children, youth, and families in poverty.

### Journal of Cognitive Rehabilitation

http://www.neuroscience.cnter.com/jcr/nsp/

A specialized online magazine containing general interest articles, personal experience articles, research reports and computerized therapy exercises related to brain injury, head injury, and strokes.

### Journal of Mind and Behavior

http://kramer.ume.maine.edu/~jmb/

Journal related to cross-causal understanding of cognition and behavior. Contents and abstracts of articles in past issues.

### The Journal of Online Behavior (JOB)

http://www.behavior.net/JOB/

*JOB* is concerned with the empirical study of human behavior in the online environment, and with the impact of evolving communication and information technology upon individuals, groups, organizations, and society. It is a peer-reviewed, behavioral science/social science journal, with editorial board members from several countries and disciplinary affiliations. The journal is published electronically on the World Wide Web, and in printed form. Each article published on the Web is accompanied by an interactive discussion space, a pointer to which will accompany the article site. Significant comments from discussions may accompany the paper publication.

### Journal of Poverty

http://www.journalofpoverty.org/

*The Journal of Poverty: Innovations on Social, Political and Economic Inequalities* is the first refereed journal designed to provide a focused outlet for discourse on poverty and inequality.

### Journal of Social Work Practice

`http://www.tandf.co.uk/journals/carfax/02650533.html`

*The Journal of Social Work Practice* publishes refereed articles devoted to the exploration and practice of social welfare and allied health professions from psychodynamic and systemic perspectives.

### Links to Psychological Journals (by Armin Gunther)

`http://www.psycline.org/journals/psycline.html`

An index of more than 1,500 links to psychology and social science journals online, this Web site covers English, French, and Dutch language journals, and provides general journal information, tables of contents, abstracts, or full text articles.

### Lippincott's Nursing Center

`http://www.nursingcenter.com/`

The *American Journal of Nursing* was the first U.S. nursing publication to make a home on the World Wide Web. It has recently launched Lippincott's NursingCenter, which features full-text continuing education articles as well as tables of contents from the current *AJN,* summaries of articles, and links to sites for other nursing journals.

### The New Social Worker

`http://www.socialworker.com/`

*The New Social Worker* is the only national magazine devoted to social work students and recent graduates. This Web site presents the online version of the magazine, and presents links to employment resources.

### NIH Record

`http://www.nih.gov/news/NIH-Record/archives.htm`

*The NIH Record* is the biweekly newsletter for employees of the National Institutes of Health.

### On the Issues: The Progressive Woman's Quarterly

http://mosaic.echonyc.com/~onissues/

This Internet-only journal presents articles on international and domestic affairs, political analysis, philosophy, religion and spirituality, health and medicine, arts, culture, social and personal issues.

### Philanthropy News Digest

http://fdncenter.org/pnd/current/

The Foundation Center publishes electronically its *Philanthropy News Digest* every week, highlighting philanthropy-related news from other print and electronic periodicals nationwide.

### Proceedings of the National Academy of Sciences

http://www.pnas.org/

PNAS is one of the world's most-cited multidisciplinary scientific serials. Since its establishment in 1915, it continues to publish cutting-edge research reports, commentaries, reviews, perspectives, colloquium papers, and actions of the Academy. Coverage in PNAS spans the biological, physical, and social sciences. PNAS is published biweekly in print, and weekly online in PNAS Early Edition.

### Psychiatric Times

http://www.mhsource.com/psychiatrictimes.html

Full text of news and clinical articles for psychiatrists, allied mental health professionals and primary care physicians who treat mental disorders.

### Psychiatry on Line

http://www.priory.co.uk/psycont.htm

Current contents and more from the *International Journal of Psychiatry*.

### Psychotherapy Finances and Managed Care Strategies

http://www.psyfin.com

Two newsletters related to subjects private practitioners and those in managed care need to know about: practice building; marketing tips; hot niche market opportunities; health reform initiatives; plus managed care news and even tax tips.

### PSYCHE

`http://psyche.cs.monash.edu.au/`

A refereed electronic journal dedicated to supporting the interdisciplinary exploration of the nature of consciousness and its relation to the brain.

### Psychological Science Agenda

`http://www.apa.org/psa/psacover.html`

The newsletter of the American Psychological Association Science Directorate.

### Psycoloquy

`http://www.princeton.edu/~harnad/psyc.html`

A refereed international, interdisciplinary electronic journal sponsored by the American Psychological Association (APA), publishing target articles and peer commentary in all areas of psychology as well as cognitive science, neuroscience, behavioral biology, artificial intelligence, robotics/vision, linguistics and philosophy.

### Qualitative Report

`http://www.nova.edu/ssss/QR/`

An online journal dedicated to qualitative research and critical inquiry.

### Social Policy

`http://www.socialpolicy.org/`

Electronic magazine about social and political movements and issues. Provides articles, a message board, and links to related resources.

### Social Research Update

`http://www.soc.surrey.ac.uk/sru/`

A quarterly publication by the Department of Sociology, University of Surrey, England. Each issue covers one topic in sufficient depth to indicate the main directions of recent developments and provide a bibliography for further reading.

### Social Service Review

`http://www.journals.uchicago.edu/SSR/`

Contents, author notes, and full-text articles from one of the premier journals in social work.

### Sociological Research Online

http://www.socresonline.org.uk/

Online journal that publishes peer reviewed articles applying sociological analysis to a wide range of topics.

### Standards: An International Journal of Multicultural Studies

http://www.colorado.edu/journals/standards/

An online publication featuring art, fiction, and scholarly essays relating to multicultural studies.

### Technology in Human Services

http://www2.uta.edu/cussn/jths/

Technology in Human Services is a journal dedicated to providing information about the use of computer-based information technologies in the human services. It is designed for practitioners as well as educators.

## Social Work Areas of Practice Sites

### ADMINISTRATION

### Action Without Borders

http://www.idealist.org/

Organization with an aim to create a global network of community-based centers that will link, serve, and strengthen individuals and organizations working to build a better world.

### Aspen Institute

http://www.aspeninst.org/

This site offers information on the activities and programs of the Aspen Institute in the U.S. and in Germany, France, Italy and Japan. The Aspen Institute is dedicated to the development of leadership in the nonprofit sector.

### Best Practices Toolkit

http://www.benton.org/Practice/Toolkit/

This is a list of Internet and other resources aimed at helping nonprofits make better use of information and communications technologies in their work.

### Council on Foundations

`http://www.cof.org/`

Features information on the Council, which is dedicated to assisting grant-makers become more effective fundraisers and to supporting the growth of organized philanthropy.

### Foundation Center

`http://fdncenter.org/`

A nonprofit information clearinghouse, providing information on foundations and corporate giving. The Center's site includes information on the Center, its libraries, seminars and publications. The site also features grant-maker information (including links to grantmaker Web sites), a searchable database of philanthropy-related articles, and a section on the fundraising process, including a proposal writing short course.

### Free Management Library

`http://www.mapnp.org/library/`

The Free Management Library (formerly the Nonprofit Managers' Library) facilitates sharing of free, online, and how-to management resources among nonprofits—including fundraising and grant writing, marketing and public relations, using the Internet, and evaluation. The Management Assistance Program (MAP) for Nonprofits in St. Paul, Minnesota administers the library.

### GuideStar

`http://www.guidestar.org/`

Information on the programs and finances of more than 700,000 American nonprofits organizations, with up-to-date news stories and features on philanthropy, and a forum for donors and volunteers.

### Impact Online

`http://www.impactonline.org/`

A new organization that encourages community involvement by offering information on the Web about nonprofits with additional components for fundraising and volunteering.

### Independent Sector

`http://www.indepsec.org/`

Presents the various aspects of Independent Sector, a national coalition of voluntary organizations, foundations, and corporate giving programs, including information on Independent Sector's advocacy, research, and leadership programs.

### Internet Nonprofit Center

`http://www.nonprofits.org/`

The site features the Nonprofit Locater, offering access to the IRS' Business Master File, which provides information on each charity in the Business Master File, including assets and revenues. The Center's site also offers a library of publications on nonprofits, a feature on the Top 40 Charities, and information on evaluating nonprofits and standards in philanthropy.

### Introducing New Technology Successfully into an Agency

`http://www.coyotecom.com/database/techbuy.html`

Introducing computers to your agency, or upgrading software or hardware your agency uses, will change the way you access and manage information—for the better, you hope. But without realistic expectations and a thoughtful strategy, a new system can create as many problems as it is supposed to solve. This tip sheet can help.

### The Joseph and Matthew Payton Philanthropic Studies Library

`http://www-lib.iupui.edu/special/ppsl.html`

The mission of the philanthropic studies collection is to support the educational and research programs of the Indiana University Center on Philanthropy.

### The Management Assistance Program for Nonprofits

`http://www.mapnp.org/`

MAP for Nonprofits primarily works with nonprofit organizations in the Greater Twin Cities Metropolitan Area of Minneapolis and St. Paul. Their Web site contains information about services they provide to nonprofits and a library of information helpful to social work administrators.

### The Management Center

`http://www.tmcenter.org`

Helps nonprofit organizations manage better by providing consulting services in Northern California, conducting workshops and programs for professionals and board member, and producing a nonprofit job listing and an annual compensation survey.

### BoardSource

`http://www.boardsource.org`

Provides information on BoardSource's activities, including its training, education, and consulting services for nonprofit boards, as well as BoardSource's National Leadership Forum. The site also features a catalog of materials on nonprofit governance published by the BoardSource, and also includes a Board Information Center that provides answers and information on nonprofit governance.

### National Opportunity NOCs

`http://www.opportunitynocs.org/`

A resource for nonprofit jobs and employment opportunities. Job seekers can conduct free searches through our large database of available nonprofit jobs online, while nonprofit organizations can post help wanted classified ads for job openings online. The site also features a career center, nonprofit library and additional nonprofit employment resources.

### *Nonprofit Cyber-Accountability*

`http://www.bway.net/~hbograd/cyb-acc.html`

Offers the Cyber-Accountability listserv, an ongoing discussion on the non-profit world and the use of information technology. The site also provides information on the National Accountability Research Project at the Nonprofit Coordinating Committee of New York, as well as links to other sites that contain information on nonprofits.

### *The Non-Profit Internet Handbook*

`http://www.socialworker.com/nonprofit/npinter.htm`

The Non-Profit Internet Handbook is for nonprofit organizations that want to get the most out of the Internet. It is a valuable resource for executive staff, board members, those who donate funds, and those who contribute time to nonprofit organizations.

### *npinfotech.org—Technology Support for Nonprofit Organizations*

`http://www.npinfotech.org/`

npinfotech.org is a nonprofit organization with the mission of bringing together nonprofits and providers of information technology services and products to better the ability of nonprofits to achieve their goals and objectives. Their mission is support nonprofits by matching information services providers with nonprofits, conducting educational seminars about information technology and related topics, operating The Nonprofit Software Index, and providing information about information technology, computer software and the Internet to nonprofit organizations through a variety of media.

### *Paradigms*

`http://www.rhd.org/Paradigms/`

A virtual posting board for the nonprofit community providing an online forum to nonprofit projects, an exchange of innovations and revolutionary project strategies, and a directory of project models.

### *Philanthropy News Network Online*

`http://pnnonline.org/`

The Web site has extensive resources with alerts and links to many non-profit sites, including a Meta-Index comprehensive text list of resources on the Internet of interest to nonprofits.

### PRAXIS

`http://www.ssw.upenn.edu/~restes/praxis.html`

Resources for social and economic development; pointers to many resources created by Dr. Richard J. Estes at the University of Pennsylvania.

### Strategic Planning (in nonprofit or for-profit organizations)

`http://www.mapnp.org/library/plan_dec/`
`str_plan/str_plan.htm`

Sponsored by The Management Assistance Program for Nonprofits in Minneapolis, this site provides an overview of a variety of perspectives about strategic planning and a variety of approaches used in the strategic planning. The site also includes guidelines for the reader to carry out planning according to the nature and needs of their organization. The MAP provides technology grants to nonprofit organizations, and the site includes a useful section on technology planning.

### TechFoundation—Technology for Nonprofits

`http://techfoundation.org/`

TechFoundation is a new public charity whose mission is to bridge the Nonprofit Digital Divide by providing nonprofits with access to the technology, expertise, and capital they need to build a better tomorrow.

### Urban Institute

`http://www.urban.org/`

Provides information on the activities of the Institute and its research and policy centers, and programs. The site also presents briefings on topical issues.

## AGING

### Administration on Aging

`http://www.aoa.dhhs.gov/`

Information about the Administration on Aging and its programs for the elderly, information about resources for practitioners who serve the aged, statistical information on the aging, and information for consumers (older persons and their families) including how to obtain services for senior citizens and electronic booklets on aging related issues. It also includes a link to AoA's National Aging Information Center and extensive links to other aging related Web resources.

### Alzheimer's Association

http://www.alz.org/

The home page of the Alzheimer's association in the United States. Contains information about chapters, caregiver resources, medical information, public policy, and links to other resources.

### Alzheimer's Disease Resource Page

http://www.ohioalzcenter.org/resource.html

Hosted by Case Western Reserve University, this page provides information on Alzheimer's disease, for caregivers, practitioners, researchers, and the general public.

### The ALZHEIMER Page

http://www.adrc.wustl.edu/alzheimer/

A service of the Washington University (St. Louis) Alzheimer's Disease Research Center, this page provides links to just about everything you'd want to know about Alzheimer's disease.

### ALZwell Caregiver Support

http://www.alzwell.com/

ALZwell Caregiver Support is dedicated to helping dementia caregivers to find understanding, wisdom and support throughout the caregiving journey.

### APA Division 20

http://aging.ufl.edu/apadiv20/apadiv20.htm

The home page of Division 20 of the American Psychological Association (Adult Development and Aging). This site provides information about the mission of Division 20, research and employment opportunities, pre- and post-doctoral programs of study in adult development and aging, instructional resources for teachers of adult development and aging, directory of members, contact information for specific laboratories/centers and institutes, and a Resource Guide for Clinicians.

### Association for Gerontology Education in Social Work: AGE-SW

http://www.agesocialwork.org/

Provides information about the organization, gerontology-related resources, and highlights from *AGEnda,* the AGE-SW newsletter.

### DeathNET

http://www.rights.org/deathnet/

Very flashy Web site specializing in information concerning: euthanasia, suicide, assisted suicide, living wills, patient's rights, terminal illnesses such as ALS, cancer, multiple sclerosis, AIDS, heart disease, among others; hospice care, palliative care; "right to die" legislation; "self-deliverance"; and other aspects of death and dying. Also houses archives of Dr. Jack Kevorkian, Derek Humphry, right to die, and dying with dignity themes. Fortunately, there is a low-bandwidth version available for the technologically impaired.

### ElderCare Online

http://www.ec-online.net/

ElderCare Online is for people caring for aging loved ones. They are committed to providing an online community where supportive peers and professionals help improve quality of life for caregivers and their elder. Includes newsletter, discussion forums, and helpful information.

### Family Caregiver Alliance

http://www.caregiver.org/

Information about the Family Caregiver Alliance, resource centers in California, caregiver tips, statistics and research, public policy, information about educational programs and conferences, publications, and more.

### Geropsychology Central

http://www.premier.net/~gero/geropsyc.html

Devoted to the study of the neurological, psychological, sociological aspects of the aging process. Designed for the gerontology professional, seniors, and caregivers, features and links are topically organized for quick reference.

### Grand Times

http://www.grandtimes.com/mags/

An online magazine for active retirees.

### Michigan Alzheimer's Disease Research Center

http://www.med.umich.edu/madrc/

Provides information about the activities of the MADRC, their research projects, publications, programs for patients and families, and links to other Alzheimer's centers and programs and resources.

### Multidisciplinary Education in Geriatrics and Aging

```
http://cpmcnet.columbia.edu/dept/dental/
Dental_Educational_Software/
Gerontology_and_Geriatric_Dentistry/introduction.html
```

Web-based course in aging for clinicians. Excellent resource.

### National Council on Aging

```
http://www.ncoa.org/
```

An association of more than 7,500 members who work with, for, and on behalf of older persons. The organization is devoted "to promoting the dignity, self-determination, well-being, and contributions of older persons and to enhancing the field of aging through leadership and service, education, and advocacy . . . "

### Senior Net

```
http://www.seniornet.org/
```

SeniorNet is a national nonprofit organization whose mission is to build a community of computer-using senior citizens. The site contains all kinds of information for and about seniors, instructional information on computing, and message boards and chat to enable seniors to contact each other.

### Senior Sites

```
http://www.seniorsites.com/
```

This site may be the most comprehensive Web source of nonprofit housing and services for seniors. With over 5000 listed communities, Senior Sites is a valuable resource for seniors and their families interested in exploring the nonprofit housing option.

### The University of Georgia Gerontology Center

```
http://www.geron.uga.edu/
```

Highlights the activities of the center, and provides links to other resources, including aging-related grants information.

## CHILDREN, ADOLESCENTS, AND FAMILIES

### Adolescent Directory Online

`http://education.indiana.edu/cas/adol/welcome.html`

Adolescence Directory Online (ADOL) is an electronic guide to information on adolescent issues. It is a service of the Center for Adolescent Studies at Indiana University. Educators, counselors, parents, researchers, health practitioners, and teens can use ADOL to find Web resources on conflict and violence, mental health issues, health issues, counselor resources, and even help with homework.

### American Academy of Child and Adolescent Psychiatry

`http://www.aacap.org/`

AACAP is a dynamic organization, giving direction to and responding quickly to new developments in health care, and addressing the needs of children, adolescents and families. Resources are provided to educate parents and families about psychiatric disorders affecting children and adolescents.

### Casa de los Niños

`http://www.casadelosninos.org/`

The mission of Casa de los Niños is the prevention, intervention, and treatment of child abuse and neglect by providing: residential shelter care for children who are abused, neglected, or homeless; supportive counseling to families; and community education. The Web site features information about the organization, child abuse statistics, information for parents, and links to related resources.

### Center for Adolescent Studies

`http://education.indiana.edu/cas/`

The Center for Adolescent Studies at Indiana University focuses on meeting the social and emotional growth and development needs of adolescents through providing support to adults working with youth, investigating current social issues and providing tools for teens to learn and practice new, healthy behaviors. Links are provided to Center programs, which include research projects, support for teachers, and a computer-based decision aide to help schools select the drug prevention program most likely to meet their needs.

### Child Welfare

`http://www.childwelfare.com/`

Provides a gateway to information related to the welfare of children, and an electronic journal, Child Welfare Review, a library, a resource on issues related to sources on child welfare. It also features a directory of email addresses for social work faculty.

### Child Welfare League of America

`http://www.cwla.org/`

The Child Welfare League of America is the nation's oldest and largest organization devoted entirely to the well-being of America's vulnerable children and their families. The site provides information about the CWLA, advocacy tips, action alerts, and child welfare statistics.

### Children Now

`http://www.childrennow.org/`

Children Now is a nonpartisan, independent voice for children, working to translate the nation's commitment to children and families into action. The site provides access to Children Now publications, poll results, policy papers, press materials, action updates on federal and state legislation, and links to other Web sites devoted to children's issues. Users who subscribe to Children Now's Internet Digest receive online updates on children's issues.

### Children's Defense Fund

`http://www.childrensdefense.org/`

The Children's Defense Fund exists to provide a strong and effective voice for all the children of America, who cannot vote, lobby, or speak for themselves. The site provides information about the activities of the CDF, issues, news and reports, the Black Community Crusade for Children, Stand for Children, and links to related resources.

### Family.Com

`http://family.go.com/`

From Disney.com, Family.com is a service for parents offering comprehensive, high-quality, customizable information for raising children. Glitzy, but worth a visit.

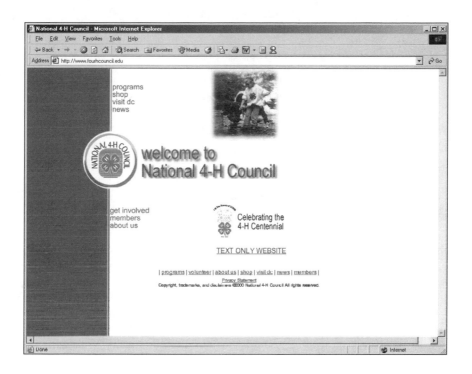

### National 4-H Council

http://www.fourhcouncil.edu/

National 4-H Council is a not-for-profit educational organization devoted to creating exciting programs and opportunities for young people. The site presents information about the organization and its activities.

### National Network for Youth

http://www.NN4Youth.org/

The National Network for Youth informs public policy, educates the public and contributes to the field of youth work. The Web site provides information for youth work advocacy and links to other resources.

### National Parent Information Network

http://npin.org/

The purpose of NPIN is to provide information to parents and those who work with parents and to foster the exchange of parenting materials.

### Parents Place.com

http://www.parentsplace.com/

The first parenting community on the Web. Provides parenting literature, advice columns, chat, bulletin boards, and shopping.

### State of the World's Children—2001

http://www.unicef.org/sowc01/

UNICEF's award-winning site presents a snapshot of the world's children in 2001, including children in war, statistical tables, regional spotlights, and references.

### YouthNet UK

http://www.thesite.org/

This UK site provides a wealth of information for youths about everything ranging from relationships to housing, and with links to virtually any subject that conceivably could be of interest to adolescents.

### YO! Youth Outlook

http://www.youthoutlook.org

YO! Youth Outlook is an award-winning monthly publication by and for young people who have stories to share. Featuring in-depth reporting pieces and first-person essays, comic strips and poetry pages, YO! is the communication outlet for youths who feel their voice and visions need to be seen and heard. YO! is a bridge to the world of youth expression.

### Youth and Children Resources Net

http://www.child.net/

Maintained by the National Children's Coalition with sponsorship from Streetcats Foundation, this page aspires to be a megasite. It provides links to news, information, resources and referrals for and about kids and teens on the World Wide Web.

## CLINICAL SOCIAL WORK PRACTICE

### APsa: The American Psychoanalytic Association

http://www.apsa.org/

Home page of the American Psychoanalytic Association.

### Behaviour Analysis

http://server.bmod.athabascau.ca/html/aupr/ba.shtml

Maintained by Athabasca University, this is believed to be the largest list of Web-based behavior-analysis resources on the Internet.

### Behavior OnLine

http://www.behavior.net/

Behavior OnLine aspires to be the meeting place online for Mental Health and Applied Behavioral Science professionals. It hosts ongoing discussions on a variety of therapeutic approaches and provides links to organizations and interests groups and to other resources.

### Cognitive Therapy

http://mindstreet.com/

MindStreet is a multimedia learning program, which uses full-screen, full-motion video and consists of 5–8 hours of computer-assisted psychotherapy, plus a take-home manual with customized homework assignments for each patient. The program uses cognitive strategies for treating depression.

### Counseling Center University at Buffalo

http://ub-counseling.buffalo.edu/selfhelp.shtml

The Counseling Center Self-Help Home Page presents a wide selection of documents, Internet resources, referrals, and reading lists, all to help students with day-to-day stresses and difficult periods in their lives.

### FreudNet: The A. A. Brill Library

http://www.nypsa.org/

This server provides access to information about library services and the collection, as well as general information about psychoanalysis within the New York area and around the country.

### Gestalt Therapy

http://www.gestalt.org/

The Gestalt Therapy Page, the Internet resource center for Gestalt therapy, includes a worldwide directory of Gestalt therapists, a Gestalt bibliography, a News at Notes bulletin board, and articles relating to Gestalt therapy.

### GrassRoots

`http://www.enabling.org/grassroots/`

GrassRoots is an online, text-based, virtual reality community, MOO, where people from around the world can come together for support, education, and fun. This online community is being designed to accommodate the needs of persons with disabilities. GrassRoots has been created in the Multi-user Object Oriented (MOO) programming language that has two components, allowing the creation of an accessible site that is uniquely effective for social interaction and education.

### The National Institute for the Psychotherapies

`http://www.nipinst.org/`

The National Institute for the Psychotherapies (NIP) training programs enhance the capacity of mental health professionals to treat child, adolescent and adult clients. The training reflects a unique commitment to draw on a wide range of theories of psychotherapy, to support the integration of existing treatment modalities, and to develop new treatment approaches.

### NetPsych.com

`http://netpsych.com/`

This site explores the new uses of the Internet to deliver Psychological and Healthcare Services. NetPsych is the first site to focus exclusively on online resources. "HUH?" is a great button.

### Practicing Psychotherapy on the Internet: Risk Management and Great Opportunity

`http://telehealth.net/articles/njpa.html`

Written by Marlene M. Maheu, Ph.D., discusses barriers to using the Internet for psychotherapy, including confidentiality, duty to warn dilemmas, and other concerns.

### Support Coalition: Human Rights and Psychiatry Home Page

`http://www.MindFreedom.org/`

The Support Coalition is dedicated to exposing human rights abuses by the psychiatry profession.

## COMMUNITY ORGANIZATIONS

### *Campus Outreach Opportunity League*

http://www.cool2serve.org/

Founded in 1984, the Campus Outreach Opportunity League (COOL) is a national nonprofit that helps college students start, strengthen, and expand their community service programs.

### *The Center for Civic Networking*

http://www.civic.net/ccn.html

The Center for Civic Networking (CCN) is a nonprofit organization dedicated to applying information infrastructure to the broad public good—particularly by putting information infrastructure to work within local communities to improve delivery of local government services, improving access to information that people need in order to function as informed citizens, broadening citizen participation in governance, and stimulating economic and community development. Among the topics covered on the site are issues related to community building on the Internet and Internet access for the poor.

### *Civic Practices Network*

http://www.cpn.org

CPN is a collaborative and nonpartisan project bringing together a diverse array of organizations and perspectives within the citizen participation movement.

### *The Community Builders Fellowship*

http://www.hud.gov/cb/cbhome.html

A program of the US Department of Housing and Urban Development, in partnership with Harvard University's John F. Kennedy School of Government, the purpose of the Community Builders Fellowship program to educate and train individuals from diverse professions as Community Builders. As Community Builders, individuals can obtain practical, hands-on experience in community and economic development during a two-to-four year stay with HUD.

### *Community Networking Documents and Resources*

http://www.ifla.org/II/commun.htm

This site offers links to a variety of Internet resources related to Internet access and community-building.

### Community Networks: An Online Guide to Resources

`http://mason.gmu.edu/~pbaker/1cnindex.html`

This Web site is a compilation of references, links, and publications related to a variety of networked information infrastructures.

### The Digital Divide Network

`http://www.digitaldividenetwork.org/`

There has always been a gap between those people and communities who can make effective use of information technology and those who cannot. Now, more than ever, unequal adoption of technology excludes many from reaping the fruits of the economy. At the Digital Divide Network, the digital divide is examined from many perspectives. The Web site offers a range of information, tools and resources that help practitioners stay on top of digital divide developments. It also serves as forum where practitioners can share their experiences with colleagues around the world. They examine the causes and effects of the divide from four distinct angles: technology access, literacy and learning, content, and economic development.

### HandsNet

`http://www.handsnet.org/`

HandsNet is a national, nonprofit organization that promotes information sharing, cross-sector collaboration and advocacy among individuals and organizations working on a broad range of public interest issues.

### How to Use the Internet for Organizing

`http://www.nonviolence.org/support/`

Martin Kelley, of The Nonviolence Web, has compiled "How to Use the Internet for Organizing" that can be useful to almost any organization.

### Idealist

`http://www.idealist.org/`

Idealist is a fully interactive system that enables any nonprofit or community organization– whether it has a Web site or not-to enter and update detailed information about its services, volunteer opportunities, internships, job openings, upcoming events, and any material or publication it has produced. 22,000 organizations in 150 countries are already using Idealist.

*Research Navigator Guide: Helping Professions*

### MoveOn.org

`http://www.moveon.org/`

MoveOn was started by Joan Blades and Wes Boyd, two Silicon Valley entrepreneurs, with their family and friends. MoveOn is working to bring ordinary people back into politics. Charging that the system today revolves around big money and big media, and that most citizens are left out. MoveOn is a catalyst for a new kind of grassroots involvement, supporting busy but concerned citizens in finding their political voice. MoveOn builds electronic advocacy groups around issues such as campaign finance, environmental and energy issues, impeachment, gun safety, and nuclear disarmament. MoveOn provides information and tools to help each individual have the greatest possible impact. During impeachment of President Clinton, for example, MoveOn's grassroots advocates generated more than 250,000 phone calls and a million emails to Congress.

### National Urban League

`http://www.nul.org`

The mission of the National Urban League is to assist African Americans in the achievement of social and economic equality. The Board of Trustees of the National Urban League and all of its affiliates reflect a diverse body of community, government, and corporate leaders. The League implements its mission through advocacy, bridge building, program services, and research.

### Neighborhoods Online

`http://neighborhoodsonline.net/`

Neighborhoods Online was created in 1995 by the Institute for the Study of Civic Values as an online resource center for people working to build strong communities throughout the United States. Their aim is to provide fast access to information and ideas covering all aspects of neighborhood revitalization, as well as to create a national network of neighborhood activists. The site offers information related to community development, education, crime, jobs, environment, health, and human services.

### NetAction Internet Resources

`http://www.netaction.org/resources.html`

This is a wonderful list of annotated links. Virtually everything you need to know to be a community activist using the Internet.

Research Navigator Guide: Helping Professions

### Nurturing Neighborhood Nets

`http://web.mit.edu/techreview/www/articles/`
`oct97/chapman.html`

Interesting article about how providing free access to computer networking can extend the pleasures and benefits of the Net to people living in poor communities. Provides links to several community organization efforts utilizing Internet resources.

### People-Link

`http://www.People-Link.com/`

People Link provides integrated communications to the progressive, socially responsible business, and organized labor communities. The site offers progressive and alternative news media, labor union sites and information, links to socially responsible businesses, information on environmental issues, left wing activities, women, gays and lesbians, people of color, and progressive arts.

### Smart Communities

`http://smartcommunities.ic.gc.ca/`

A Smart Community is a community with a vision of the future that involves the use of information and communication technologies in new and innovative ways to empower its residents, institutions and regions as a whole. As such, they make the most of the opportunities that new technologies afford—better health care delivery, better education and training and new business opportunities. The site profiles several models of smart communities.

### Social Contract Project

`http://neighborhoodsonline.net/socialcontract.html`

Through the Social Contract Project, the Institute for the Study of Civic Values has developed a new way for neighborhood activists, business leaders, and public officials to develop comprehensive plans for neighborhood improvement. These stakeholders negotiate an explicit social contract defining how they will work together to make the neighborhood is clean, safe, economically viable, and a decent place to raise children. The site details the work of the project.

## DISABILITIES

### Ability

http://www.ability.org.uk/

Ability is a grassroots organization in the UK that is dedicated to utilizing computer technology and the Internet for people with disabilities. The site offers access to disability and health resources, social contacts, message boards, classified ads, and news.

### Active Living Alliance

http://www.ala.ca/

The Active Living Alliance for Canadians with a Disability is a partnership of 17 National Associations whose common goal is to facilitate active living opportunities for Canadians with a disability. Information about the alliance, news, and links to related resources are offered.

### The Kansas Commission on Disability Concerns

http://adabbs.hr.state.ks.us/dc/

This site offers a wealth of information and resources for people with disabilities in Kansas, nationally and internationally.

### American Council for the Blind

http://www.acb.org/

This site offers information about the activities of the organization, recent issues of its monthly publications, and helpful resources and information about blindness.

### American Foundation for the Blind

http://www.afb.org/

Information about the AFB, the *Journal of Visual Impairment and Blindness,* the AFB Press Catalog, the Helen Keller photograph collection, and information on blindness, low vision and related issues.

### The Archimedes Project

http://archimedes.stanford.edu/

The mission of the Archimedes Project is to help secure equality of access to information for individuals with disabilities through the development of computer technology and the promulgation of knowledge about disability to present and future designers in academia and industry.

### The ARC

http://TheArc.org

The Arc (formerly Association for Retarded Citizens of the United States) is the country's largest voluntary organization committed to the welfare of all children and adults with mental retardation and their families.

### Associated Services for the Blind

http://www.asb.org

This site offers information about the organization's services and information about subscribing to popular national magazines on cassette.

### Attention Deficit Disorder

http://www.pilgrims.net/plymouth/schools/Links/SPED/ADD.html

A project of the Plymouth, Massachusetts public schools, this page provides a wealth of Internet resources related to attention deficit disorder.

### The British Dyslexia Association

http://www.bda-dyslexia.org.uk/

The BDA sponsors the Dyslexia Archive, which is an ever-growing collection of up-to-date material covering all aspects of dyslexia.

### Center for Computer Assistance to the Disabled

http://www.c-cad.org/

CCAD is a nonprofit organization whose mission is "enhancing the quality of life and employment options of persons with disabilities through the use of modified personal computers, adaptive devices, and custom software."

### The Center for Independent Living

http://www.cilberkeley.org/

The Center for Independent Living (CIL) is a national leader in helping people with disabilities live independently and become productive, fully participating members of society.

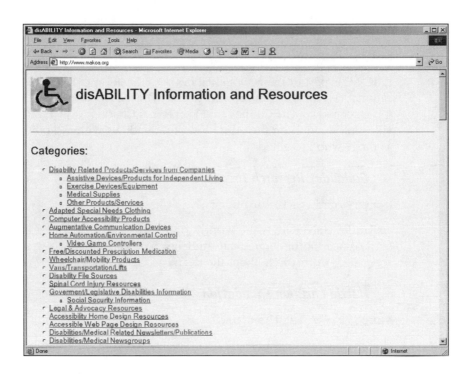

### disABILITY Information and Resources

`http://www.makoa.org/`

One of the largest collections of resources for all types of disabilities.

### Disabled Peoples' International

`http://www.dpi.org`

The purpose of DPI is to promote the Human Rights of People with Disabilities through full participation, equalization of opportunity and development. DPI is a grassroots, cross-disability network with member organizations in more than 120 countries, over half of which are in the developing world. DPI is administrated through the headquarters in Winnipeg, Canada and through eight Regional Development Offices. DPI has consultative status with the ECOSOC, UNESCO, WHO, and the ILO, and has official observer status at the United Nations General Assembly.

### Down Syndrome WWW Page

`http://www.nas.com/downsyn/`

A support and information page for parents, professionals and others interested in Down syndrome.

### ERIC Clearinghouse on Disabilities and Gifted Education

`http://ericec.org`

ERIC EC is part of the National Library of Education (NLE), Office of Educational Research and Improvement (OERI), U.S. Department of Education. It is operated by The Council for Exceptional Children (CEC). ERIC EC provides information on the education of individuals with disabilities as well as those who are gifted.

### Gallaudet Research Institute

`http://gri.gallaudet.edu/`

Gallaudet University is the world's only four-year university for deaf and hard of hearing undergraduate students. The Gallaudet Research Institute specializes in research about the deaf.

### Hattie Larlham Foundation

`http://www.larlham.org/`

HLF is a private, nonprofit service agency for young people with mental retardation, developmental disabilities and/or complex medical needs. The Web site is offered as a service for the families of children with profound disabilities, professionals who work with children having disabilities and anyone who wishes to learn more.

### Hearing Loss Resources

`http://www.saywhatclub.com`

The SayWhatClub sponsors the Hearing Loss Resources Web site. Internet mailing lists and nonprofit organizations that focus on the issue of hearing loss are featured.

### International Center for Disability Resources on the Internet

`http://www.icdri.org/`

The Center's mission is to collect and present as many disability-related Internet resources as there are available, including resources directly related to disabilities and other resources that may be helpful to the disability community. These resources are presented in a manner that is accessible to a wide and varied audience. The Center's scope is international.

*Research Navigator Guide: Helping Professions*

### LD OnLine

http://www.ldonline.org/

An interactive guide to learning disabilities for parents, teachers and children, LD OnLine offers links to resources, including research, information, referrals, bulletin boards, chats, and more.

### National Federation of the Blind

http://www.nfb.org/

The goal of the NFB involves the removal of legal, economic, and social discriminations; the education of the public to new concepts concerning blindness; and the achievement by all blind people of the right to exercise to the fullest their individual talents and capacities.

### National Library Service for the Blind and Physically Handicapped

http://lcweb.loc.gov/nls/

The Library of Congress a free library program of Braille and recorded materials circulated to eligible borrowers through a network of cooperating libraries. This Web site offers access to online catalogs of holdings.

### National Technical Institute for the Deaf

http://ntidweb.rit.edu/

One of the seven colleges of the Rochester Institute of Technology (RIT), NTID is the world's first and largest technological college for deaf students. It represents the first concerted effort to educate large numbers of deaf students within a college campus planned principally for hearing students.

### Shriver Center

http://www.umassmed.edu/shriver

The Eunice Kennedy Shriver Center for Mental Retardation, Inc. is a not-for-profit service, training and research institute. The site offers information about their research, training, and services divisions.

### Values into Action

http://www.viauk.org/

VIA is a nonprofit organization that works to promote the rights of people with learning difficulties. The site offers information to promote the civil rights of people with disabilities.

### World Information on Disability

```
http://www.sd.soft.iwate-pu.ac.jp/
sensui/foreign_res.html
```

This is a Japanese site that pulls together a variety of resources on disabilities.

## DIVERSITY

### The African World Community Network

```
http://www.he.net/~awe/
```

Links to Afrocentric resources around the Internet.

### Asian American Resources

```
http://www.ai.mit.edu/people/irie/aar/
```

Provides a variety of links to Internet resources about Asian Americans.

### Asian Studies WWW Monitor

```
http://coombs.anu.edu.au/asia-www-monitor.html
```

This online newsletter was established to provide resources that are inspected and rated in terms of the quality, overall reliability and usefulness of their content to the social sciences' research in Asia-Pacific region.

### The Amistad Research Center

```
http://www.tulane.edu/~amistad/
```

An independent archives, library, and museum dedicated to preserving African-American and ethnic history and culture, housed at Tulane University.

### The African American Home Page

```
http://www.aahp.com/
```

Links to African American resources, including one of the largest collections of African American art on the Internet. Also includes recipes, bulletin boards, library resources, and links to related sites.

### The Chicano/Latino Electronic Network

```
http://latino.sscnet.ucla.edu/
```

CLNet is an emerging digital library on Latinas/os in the United States and a joint project of the Center for Virtual Research in the College of Human-

*Research Navigator Guide: Helping Professions*

ities, Arts, and Social Sciences at the UC Riverside, the Chicano Studies Research Library at UCLA and the Linguistic Minority Research Institute at the UC Santa Barbara.

### The Cradleboard Teaching Project

http://www.cradleboard.org/

Founded by Buffy Sainte-Marie, the Nihewan Foundation is dedicated to the development of curricula for American Indian Education. Included in this site is a comprehensive listing of links to Tribal resources across North America.

### Institute of Hispanic-Latino Cultures

http://www.dso.ufl.edu/lacasita/

Offers information for students at the University of Florida.

### LATIF.com Home

http://www.latif.com/links/

A listing of links and informational resources about Islam.

### Latin-American Network Information Center

http://info.lanic.utexas.edu/

This site is considered by some to be by far the best online resource for information about Latin America and the Caribbean.

### Minority Rights Group International

http://www.minorityrights.org/

MRG is an international non-governmental organization working to secure justice for minorities and majorities suffering discrimination and prejudice and to active the peaceful coexistence of majority and minority communities. MRG informs and warns governments, the international community, non-governmental organizations and the wider public about the situation of minorities around the world.

### Native American Resources

http://www.cowboy.net/native/

An abundance of links to Indian-focused Internet resources, including Tribes, Indian organizations, education, government, and art and culture.

### NetNoir

`http://www.netnoir.com/`

Your gateway to everything Afrocentric, Afro-Latin, Afro-Caribbean, Afro-European, continental African or African-American. Chat, play games, or read articles.

### Swagga.Com

`http://www.swagga.com/`

This site represents a compendium of links to Internet resources for African Americans.

### Tribal and Inter-Tribal Resolutions and Papers

`http://www.cwis.org/resolutions.html`

Sponsored by the Center For World Indigenous Studies and the Fourth World Documentation Project. This project is an online library of texts that record and preserve Indian struggles to regain their rightful place in the international community.

### The Universal Black Pages

http://www.ubp.com/

The Universal Black Pages is an information service that resides at the Georgia Institute of Technology but is not affiliated with the Institute. The main purpose of the UBP is to have a complete and comprehensive listing of African Diaspora related Web pages at a central site.

### UCI Southeast Asian Archive

http://pitcairn.lib.uci.edu/rrsc/sasian.html

The Archive, housed at University of California, Irvine Libraries, collects materials relating to the resettlement of Southeast Asian refugees and immigrants in the United States, the "boat people" and land refugees, and the culture and history of Cambodia, Laos, and Vietnam.

### The UCLA Asian American Studies Center

http://www.sscnet.ucla.edu/aasc/

Highlights the activities of the center, provides access to publications, and links to related resources.

### The WWW Hmong Home Page

http://www.hmongnet.org

The WWW Hmong Home Page, first made available on the Internet in March, 1994, is a volunteer effort bringing together a collection the Internet-based resources related to Hmong news and current-events, issues, history, publications, and culture. This site is an official Asian Studies WWW Virtual Library Associate site.

## GENDER

### Bookbeast's Feminist Threads Home Page

http://www.bookbeast.com/ft.htm

Offers a variety of information of interest to women, including ecofeminism, ethnic and international resources, U.S. Politics, general and reference resources, books and publications, law and freedom, religion, lesbian culture, music, art and film, health and safety, work and leisure, and notices about upcoming events.

### Feminist Activist Resources

http://www.igc.org/women/feminist.html

This guide is particularly oriented toward connecting feminists who are activists to useful resources on the Internet.

### Feminist.Com

http://feminist.com/

FEMINIST.COM is aimed at helping women network, and educating and empowering women (and men) on issues that affect their lives. Offers news, information about resources, activism, women's health, articles and speeches, women-owned businesses, and classifieds.

### Feminist Majority Foundation

http://www.feminist.org/

The Feminist Majority and The Feminist Majority Foundation are committed to empowering women and winning equality through research, the sharing of information of value to feminists everywhere, and effective action. The site offers action alerts, news and press releases, and information about events of interest.

### Feminist Theory Web Site

http://www.cddc.vt.edu/feminism/

The Feminist Theory Web site provides research materials and information for students, activists, and scholars interested in women's conditions and struggles around the world. The goals of this Web site are: 1) to encourage a wide range of research into feminist theory, and 2) to encourage dialogue between women (and men) from different countries around the world. Hopefully, this will result in new connections, new ideas, and new information about feminist theory and women's movements.

### The International Foundation for Gender Education

http://www.ifge.org/

The International Foundation for Gender Education (IFGE), founded in 1987, is a leading advocate and educational organization for promoting the self-definition and free expression of individual gender identity.

### Men's Issues Page

http://www.vix.com/men/

*Research Navigator Guide: Helping Professions*

The mission of this site is to cover the several men's movements encyclopedically. It seeks to maintain comprehensive reference lists of men's movement organizations, books, periodicals, Web links and other related resources, as well as to serve as an online reference source for statistics, studies and bibliographies of interest to the men's movements.

### Men's Movement Resources on the Web

`http://www.psychstat.smsu.edu/scripts/dws148f/`
`mensresourcesmain.asp`

David W. Stockburger has compiled a list of resources for men's issues, including organizations, literature and information, advocacy pages, and government links.

### National Organization for Women

`http://now.org/`

Official home page of the National Organization for Women. Offers information about the organization and its agenda, as well as feminism, women, abortion rights, violence against women, racial and ethnic diversity, and economic equity.

### Women.com

`http://www.women.com`

A women's network for women's content and community, includes Women's Wire, Beatrice's Web Guide, Prevention's Healthy Ideas, Stork Site, and MoneyMode, plus community forums where visitors take center stage.

### WomensNet

`http://www.igc.org/igc/gateway/wnindex.html`

WomensNet was launched in early 1995. WomensNet is an online community of individuals and organizations who use computer technology to advance the interests of women worldwide. WomensNet played a key role in disseminating information at the World Conference on Women in Beijing and to the outside world as well.

### Women's Resource Center

`http://www.Colorado.edu/StudentAffairs/`
`WomensResourceCenter/`

The Women's Resource Center at the University of Colorado, Boulder serves as a resource for the university community and an advocate for women of all backgrounds, races, classes, ages, sexual orientations, political and religious beliefs, and physical abilities.

### Women's Resources on the Web: INDEX

`http://www.polaris.net/~ratliff/emily/women.html`

Offers links related to health, safety, sexuality, sports, Women's Studies, women in technology, politics and activism, and more.

### Women's Studies (R)E-sources on the Web

`http://scriptorium.lib.duke.edu/women/cyber.html`

Lots of women's studies links. The various Internet sites listed are primarily electronic sources that may be useful for Women's Studies.

### WWWomen!

`http://www.wwwomen.com/`

Considered to be the premier search directory for women's resources on the Internet, offers both hierarchical and keyword searching.

## HEALTH

### American Medical Specialty Organization

`http://www.amso.com/`

The AMSO site offers the Managed Care Forum and information about other related health care issues. The World-Wide Healthcare Poll and Healthcare forums provide a place for the health care professional, executive, or a concerned health care consumer to read and submit ideas and information in a moderated environment.

### American Public Health Association

`http://www.apha.org/`

APHA represents more than 50,000 members from over 50 occupations of public health, bringing together researchers, health service providers, administrators, teachers, and other health workers in a unique, multidisciplinary environment of professional exchange, study, and action.

### The Canadian Health Network

`http://www.hc-sc.gc.ca/`

Information about the health care system in Canada and links to informational resources.

### CancerWEB

http://www.graylab.ac.uk/cancernet/

This cancer resource site has information available on many different aspects of cancer investigation and treatment. Especially helpful is an online medical dictionary.

### Center for Rural Health and Social Service Development

http://www.siu.edu/~crhssd/

Southern Illinois University at Carbondale's CRHSSD conducts research, needs assessments, demonstration projects, program evaluations, and training; tests new models of health care delivery; and develops policy recommendations to improve the health of our rural population.

### ChronicILLNet

http://www.chronicillnet.org/

This is the first multimedia information source on the Internet dedicated to chronic illnesses including AIDS, cancer, Gulf War Syndrome, autoimmune diseases, Chronic Fatigue Syndrome, heart disease and neurological diseases. This site offers information for researchers, patients, lay people, and physicians.

### Clinical Trials Listings

http://www.CenterWatch.com/

Center Watch is a publishing company that focuses on the clinical trials industry. Their Web site is dedicated to assisting patients and their advocates to learn about and identify ongoing clinical trials seeking study volunteers.

### Diabetes Public Health Resources

http://www.cdc.gov/diabetes/

Sponsored by the Division of Diabetes Translation, a division of the National Center for Chronic Disease Prevention and Health Promotion of the Centers for Disease Control and Prevention. The division is responsible for translating scientific research findings into health promotion, disease prevention and treatment strategies.

### Go Ask Alice!

http://www.goaskalice.columbia.edu/

Sponsored by Healthwise, the Health Education and Wellness program of the Columbia University Health Service, *Go Ask Alice!* is an interactive question and answer service, answering questions each week about health, including questions about sexuality, sexual health, relationships, general health, fitness and nutrition, emotional well-being, and alcohol and other drugs.

### The Harriet Lane Links

http://162.129.72.40/poi/

The Harriet Lane Links (formerly Pediatric Points of Interest) provide an edited collection of pediatric resources (more than 5,000 links) on the World Wide Web. Maintained and edited by physicians at the Johns Hopkins University, this site attempts to catalog, review and score existing links to pediatric information on the Internet.

### The Health Care for the Homeless Information Resource Center

http://www.prainc.com/hch/

The Health Care for the Homeless Information Resource Center offers front-line providers and program staff easy access to the most current research and information about clinical practices, funding opportunities, and legislative initiatives that impact their work. Operated for the Health Resources and Services Administration's Bureau of Primary Health Care by Policy Research Associates, Inc., the Health Care for the Homeless Information Resource Center supports the effective delivery of health care services to homeless people by providing technical assistance and targeted information.

### Healthfinder®

http://www.healthfinder.gov/

Healthfinder® is a gateway consumer health and human services information Web site from the United States government. Healthfinder® can lead you to selected online publications, clearinghouses, databases, Web sites, and support and self-help groups, as well as the government agencies and not-for-profit organizations that produce reliable information for the public. Launched in April 1997, Healthfinder® served Internet users over 1.7 million times in its first year online.

### Juvenile Diabetes Foundation

http://www.jdf.org/

The Juvenile Diabetes Foundation is a not-for-profit, voluntary health agency whose mission is to support and fund research to find a cure for diabetes and its complications. The site offers a range of diabetes information.

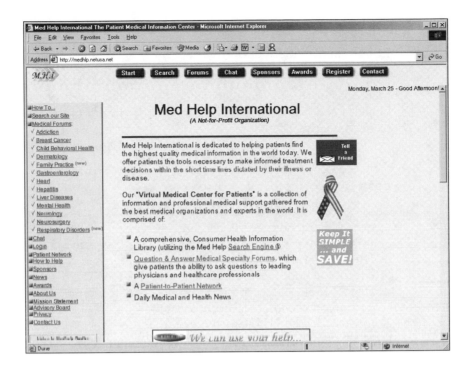

### Med Help International

`http://medhlp.netusa.net/`

Med Help International is dedicated to helping all who are in need find qualified medical information and support for their medical conditions and questions, regardless of their economic status or geographic location. Offers library searches and patient support through chat resources.

### The Minority Health Network

`http://www.pitt.edu/AFShome/e/j/ejb4/public/html/min`

MHNet is a World Wide Web based information source for individuals interested in the health of minority groups, referring to all people of color and people who are underrepresented economically and socially.

### Muscular Dystrophy Association

`http://www.mdausa.org/`

Offers links to information about MD and to related associations worldwide.

### National Center for Farmworker Health

http://www.ncfh.org/

NCFH is a private, not-for-profit corporation located in Austin, Texas. NCFH has evolved into a multi-faceted organization that provides a wide range of services dedicated to improving the health of the workers who harvest America's crops.

### National Center for Health Education

http://www.nche.org/

The National Center for Health Education (NCHE) is a nonprofit health education organization. We design and disseminate health education programs including *Growing Healthy,* America's first comprehensive school health education curriculum. *Growing Healthy* is designed to provide teachers of school health education with the tools needed to effectively teach health education. We also develop health education products that cover topics including violence prevention, drug prevention, and adolescent health issues including HIV and AIDS, sexuality education, sexually transmitted diseases (STDs), sexual abuse, and birth control and unintended pregnancy.

### Nursing Net

http://www.nursingnet.org/

NursingNet's mission is to help further the knowledge and understanding of Nursing for the public, and to provide a forum for medical professionals and students to obtain and disseminate information about nursing and medically related subjects. Offers a wide range of Internet nursing resources.

### Online Diabetes Resources

http://www.mendosa.com/faq.htm

This comprehensive directory of substantive information about diabetes provides links to important resources for diabetics.

### National Information Center on Health Services Research & Health Care Technology

http://www.nlm.nih.gov/nichsr/

NICHSR was created at the National Library of to improve the collection, storage, analysis, retrieval, and dissemination of information on health services research, clinical practice guidelines, and on health care technology, including the assessment of such technology.

### PEDINFO Home Page

http://www.pedinfo.org/

This Web server is dedicated to the dissemination of online information for pediatricians and others interested in child health.

### RxList: The Internet Drug Index

http://www.rxlist.com/

Information on commonly described drugs in both English and Spanish.

### Synapse Publishing

http://www.medlib.com/

Synapse, Inc. creates Disease Guidance Systems—medical software that uses the concept of evidence-based medicine. They are the publishers of the Cochrane Database of Systematic Reviews, Stroke: A Practical Guide to Management (Blackwell), and creators of the StrokeNet and the Stroke Guidance System. Their site offers some great resources about neuromuscular illnesses.

### WWW Virtual Library: Biosciences: Medicine

http://www.ohsu.edu/cliniweb/wwwvl/

An hierarchical listing of medical topics for finding resources on the Web.

### Y-Me National Breast Cancer Organization

http://www.y-me.org/

Y-ME National Breast Cancer Organization has a commitment to provide information and support to anyone who has been touched by breast cancer. Y-ME serves women with breast cancer and their families and friends through their national hotline, open door groups, early detection workshops and local chapters.

## HIV/AIDS

### ACT-UP NY

http://www.actupny.org/

The New York chapter of this advocacy and political action group's home page provides information about the organization, links, and an activist email list signup.

### AIDSmap

`http://www.aidsmap.com`

A very useful gateway to HIV and AIDS related information for the UK.

### AIDS Project—Los Angeles

`http://www.apla.org/`

Uses a search engine to link users to a variety of information, including services, special events, volunteer opportunities, publications, grass roots organizing, and information links.

### AIDS Resource List

`http://www.specialweb.com/aids/`

A comprehensive list of HIV/AIDS related links from Celine Chamberlin, a self-proclaimed Internet addict.

### The Body: A Multimedia AIDS and HIV Resource

`http://www.thebody.com/`

Covers many topics, including: prevention, safe sex, testing, treatment (protease inhibitors, combination therapy, viral load, azt, ddi, ddc, d4t, 3tc, reverse transcriptase), QandA w/ experts, hotlines, and politics.

### Center for AIDS Prevention Studies

`http://www.caps.ucsf.edu/`

CAPS is committed to maintaining a focus on prevention of HIV disease, using the expertise of multiple disciplines, and an applied and community-based perspective within a university setting. The Web site features information about the activities of the center, fact sheets, and a "Prevention Toolbox."

### Children with AIDS Project

`http://www.aidskids.org/`

Children with AIDS Project of America offers a variety of services for children infected/affected by AIDS or drug exposed infants who will require foster or adoptive families. The site offers information about the organization and links to other resources.

### Correctional HIV Consortium (CHC)

http://www.silcom.com/~chc/

Nonprofit corporation whose area of expertise is AIDS and HIV disease as it affects the various components of the criminal justice system and corrections communities.

### Critical Path AIDS Project

http://www.critpath.org/

The Critical Path AIDS Project was founded by persons with AIDS to provide treatment, resource and prevention information for researchers, service providers, treatment activists, but primarily for other persons with AIDS.

### Detroit Community AIDS Library

http://www.libraries.wayne.edu/dcal/aids.html

Gateway to HIV/AIDS Information for Detroit and Southeastern Michigan. Provides links to news and announcements, local AIDS service organizations, searchable databases, and HIV/AIDS Internet resources.

### Health and Law Policy Institute

http://www.law.uh.edu/healthlawperspectives/HIVAIDS/

Several papers on legal issues relating to HIV and AIDS from the University of Houston Law Center.

### HIV InSite

http://hivinsite.ucsf.edu/

Comprehensive and reliable information on HIV/AIDS treatment, policy, research, epidemiology, and prevention from the University of California, San Francisco.

### HIV Law: Paul Hampton Crockett

http://www.thebody.com/crockett/legalix.html

Paul Hampton Crockett is a partner in the law firm of Crockett & Chasen, P.A. in South Miami Beach. He and his partner specialize in the legal advice and representation of gays and lesbians, and also specialize in the large number of legal issues raised by HIV, including estate and health care planning, disability planning, insurance issues, viatical settlements, and the law of discrimination. He has served as a volunteer for ten years with the

Health Crisis Network, a community-based comprehensive AIDS services organization in Dade County, Florida, and currently sits on the organization's board of directors. This site links to a number of pages written by him about HIV law, which represent a comprehensive survival guide to the legal system for people living with HIV.

### HIVpositive.com

http://www.hivpositive.com/

The HIVpositive site offers HIV-related info on a wide-range of topics including but not limited to nutrition, treatment, caregivers, finances, and drug advisories. The mission of the site is to improve the quality of life of anyone affected in some way by the HIV virus. Among the agencies contributing information are the CDC, FDA, NIH, the Gay Men's Health Crisis, and the American Foundation for AIDS Research.

### HIV/AIDS Treatment Information

http://www.hivatis.org/

The HIV/AIDS Treatment Information Service (ATIS) provides timely, accurate treatment information on HIV and AIDS through the use of federally approved treatment guidelines and information. The HSTAT database contains the full text of approved treatment guidelines being used by the service.

### International Council of AIDS Service Organizations

http://www.icaso.org/

The ICASO network is an interactive global focus point in the international HIV/AIDS world, gathering and disseminating information and analysis on key issues, coordinating the development of CBO/NGO positions on these issues, and working as partners with key international agencies to ensure that the concerns and interests of CBOs and NGOs around the world are articulated and represented at all levels.

### Marty Howard's HIV/AIDS Home Page

http://www.smartlink.net/~martinjh/

This page is designed to help users find as much HIV/AIDS related information as possible from one starting place.

### Medscape—AIDS

http://www.medscape.com/Home/Topics/AIDS/AIDS.html

Medscape features peer-reviewed articles, zoomable color graphics, self-assessment features, medical information, medical news, free MEDLINE, CME credit, and annotated links to Internet resources.

### National Centre in HIV Social Research

http://www.arts.unsw.edu.au/nchsr/

The site documents the research activities of this Australian center.

### Pets Are Loving Support

http://www.sonic.net/~pals/

PALS is a nonprofit agency organized to improve the quality of life of people with AIDS by preserving and promoting the human/animal bond through the care and maintenance of their animal companions.

### Guide to Safer Sex

http://www.sexuality.org/safesex.html

A resource site providing information about safer sex, condoms, HIV, and contraception.

### SWEAIDS-NET

http://www.mun.ca/sweaids/sweaids.html

HIV/AIDS Social Work Education Canadian Network. The site serves as an interactive tool for sharing experiences, resources, and information social work educators, field instructors, students and trainers involved in HIV/AIDS related social work.

### UNAIDS

http://www.unaids.org/

The Joint United Nations Programme on HIV/AIDS maintains this page to disseminate information on HIV/AIDS.

### www.aidsnyc.org

http://www.aidsnyc.org/

A linked collection of pages from HIV/AIDS community-based organizations in New York City.

## HOUSING, HUNGER, AND POVERTY

### Action Aid

http://www.actionaid.org/

ACTIONAID is a leading development charity working directly with three million of the world's poorest people in Africa, Asia and Latin America, helping them in their fight against poverty.

### America's Charities

http://www.charities.org/

America's Charities goal is to provide member charities with the necessary resources to meet needs impacting human service, health and education, civil and human rights, and the environment.

### Bread for the World

http://www.bread.org/

Citizens' movement seeking justice for the world's hungry people by lobbying our nation's decision-makers.

### Education of Homeless Children and Youth

http://nch.ari.net/edchild.html

Fact sheet from the National Coalition for the Homeless. A list of resources for further study is also provided.

### Food For The Hungry: World Crisis Network

http://www.fh.org/

Food for the Hungry feeds the hungry worldwide. The site provides information about hunger and connects volunteers with sponsorship activities.

### Food Research and Action Center

http://www.frac.org/

FRAC works to improve public policies to eradicate hunger and under nutrition in the United States.

### HomeAid America

http://www.HomeAid.org/

HomeAid's mission is to build or renovate shelters for transitionally home-less men, women and children. HomeAid was created to help National Association of Home Builders—affiliated home building associations develop their own independently operated HomeAid programs to help fulfill the HomeAid mission across the nation. The Orange County site offers links to several housing-related information resources.

### Homeless in America

http://www.qvctc.commnet.edu/student/GaryOKeefe/
homeless/frame.html

Information page on who are homeless in America and why they are homeless. There is also information about support groups for the home-less and political advocacy.

### Homelessness

http://aspe.os.dhhs.gov/progsys/homeless/

Offers information about homelessness in America as well as about U.S. Department of Health and Human Services assistance programs, publica-tions, research results, and other resources.

### Hunger Notes

http://www.worldhunger.org/

Hunger Notes is an online journal sponsored by the World Hunger Edu-cation Service. Its mission is to inform the community of people interested in issues of hunger and poverty, the public, and policymakers, about the causes, extent, and efforts to end hunger and poverty in the United States and the world; to promote further understanding which integrates ethical, religious, social, economic, political, and scientific perspectives on hunger and poverty; to facilitate communication and networking among those who are working for solutions; and to promote individual and collective commitment to solutions to the hunger and poverty which confront hun-dreds of millions of the people of the world.

### HungerWeb

http://www.brown.edu/Departments/
World_Hunger_Program/

A project of the World Hunger Program, HungerWeb aims to help prevent and eradicate hunger by facilitating the free exchange of ideas and infor-mation regarding the causes of, and solutions to, hunger.

### Institute for Research on Poverty (IRP)

http://www.ssc.wisc.edu/irp/

IRP provides online publications and extensive links to poverty-related statistics and information sources.

### Joint Center for Poverty Research

http://www.jcpr.org/

The Northwestern University /University of Chicago Joint Center for Poverty Research is a national and interdisciplinary community of researchers whose work advances the understanding of what it means to be poor and live in America.

### Luxembourg Income Study

http://www.lis.ceps.lu/

The Luxembourg Income Study has four goals: (1) to test the feasibility of creating a database containing social and economic data collected in household surveys from different countries; (2) provide a method allowing researchers to use the data under restrictions required by the countries providing the data; (3) create a system that will allow research requests to be received and returned to users at remote locations; and (4) promote comparative research on the economic status of populations in different countries.

### National Center for Children in Poverty

http://cpmcnet.columbia.edu/dept/nccp/

The mission of the National Center for Children in Poverty is to identify and promote strategies that reduce the number of young children living in poverty in the United States, and that improve the life chances of the millions of children under six who are growing up poor. Center projects concentrate on early childhood care and education; child and family health; family and community support; crosscutting, multistate policy analyses; demographic and evaluation research; and communications.

### National Coalition for the Homeless

http://www.nationalhomeless.org/

The National Coalition for the Homeless is a national advocacy network of homeless persons, activists, service providers, and others committed to ending homelessness through public education, policy advocacy, grassroots organizing, and technical assistance.

*Research Navigator Guide: Helping Professions*

### National Health Care for the Homeless Council, Inc.

http://www.nhchc.org/

Membership organization of health care providers working to help bring about reform of the health care system to best serve the needs of people who are homeless.

### North Carolina Welfare Resource Exchange

http://www.ncwre.org/

The North Carolina Welfare Resource Exchange (WRE) shares credible, reliable, and practical information on welfare resources and promising practices to North Carolina agencies and organizations in order to enhance the quality of services they provide to the State's low-income families and individuals.

### Northwest Harvest

http://www.northwestharvest.org/

Northwest Harvest collects and distributes food to approximately 280 hunger programs in Washington State without tax dollars or fees of any kind. In an average month, 500,000 services are provided to individuals and families in need. Nearly half of these services go to children.

### Poverty and Sustainable Livelihoods

http://www.undp.org/seped/

Research, statistics and publications on poverty and sustainable livelihoods from the United Nations Development Programme.

### Real Change

http://www.realchangenews.org/

Real Change is a newspaper for the homeless of Seattle, Washington. Highlights of recent issues are featured on this page.

### RESULTS: Ending Hunger and Poverty

http://www.resultsusa.org

RESULTS is a nonprofit, grassroots citizen's lobby that identifies sustainable solutions to the problems of hunger and poverty, nationally and worldwide, and works to generate the resources necessary to make those solutions succeed. The site features information about the organization, action alerts, background on hunger and poverty issues, Capitol updates, articles about the organization, and links to other Web sites.

### World Hunger Year

http://www.worldhungeryear.org/

Founded by Harry Chapin in 1975, WHY focuses attention on hunger and poverty and the grassroots initiatives that fight them.

## MENTAL HEALTH

### At Health Home Page

http://www.athealth.com/

At Health provides mental health information, resources, a directory of licensed psychiatrists, psychologists, counselors and other therapists, and continuing education information.

### Autism/PDD Resources Network

http://www.autism-pdd.net/

The purpose of the site is to guide users to key issues associated with Autism Spectrum disorders.

### Bereavement Resources

http://www.funeral.net/

A variety of resources for mourners.

### Center for Mental Health Services

http://www.mentalhealth.org/cmhs/

The Center for Mental Health Services (CMHS) leads Federal efforts to treat mental illnesses by promoting mental health and by preventing the development or worsening of mental illness when possible. CMHS was established under the 1992 ADAMHA Reorganization Act, Public Law 102-321, which mandates CMHS' leadership role in delivering mental health services, generating and applying new knowledge, and establishing national mental health policy. CMHS is a component of the Substance Abuse and Mental Health Services Administration, U.S. Department of Health and Human Services.

### Children and Adults with Attention Deficit Disorder

http://www.chadd.org/

C.H.A.D.D. is a nonprofit parent-based organization formed to better the lives of individuals with attention deficit disorders and those who care for them through family support and advocacy, public and professional education and encouragement of scientific research.

### Computers in Mental Health

`http://www.ex.ac.uk/cimh/`

The site is run by the Computers in Psychiatry group of the Royal College of Psychiatrists in association with InterPsych, and is maintained by Dr. Martin Briscoe, University of Exeter. The site aims to encourage the development of useful computing applications in the field of mental health. There is an associated discussion list, which is open to professionals with an interest in computing and mental health.

### Crisis, Grief, and Healing

`http://www.webhealing.com/`

This page is meant to be a place men and women can browse to understand and honor the many different paths to heal strong emotions.

### David Baldwin's Trauma Information Pages

`http://www.trauma-pages.com/`

The Trauma Information Pages focus primarily on emotional trauma and traumatic stress, including PTSD (Post-traumatic Stress Disorder), whether following individual traumatic experience(s) or a large-scale disaster. New information is added to this site about once a month. The purpose of this award-winning site is to provide information about traumatic stress for clinicians and researchers in the field.

### Dr. Grohol's Mental Health Page

`http://www.grohol.com/`

Extensive collection of articles, commentaries, and lists pertaining to mental health, for those interested in psychological self-help. Includes original articles and editorials on current issues in the field, consumer-oriented advice.

### False Memory Syndrome Facts

`http://fmsf.com/`

This site offers pointers to key resources about "false memory syndrome," dissociation, delayed recall, repression, and recovered memories of child abuse and other traumatic events.

### Memory and Reality: The False Memory Syndrome Foundation

http://www.fmsfonline.org/

The FMS Foundation is a nonprofit organization that is devoted to seeking the reasons for the spread of False Memory Syndrome; to working for the prevention of new cases of False Memory Syndrome; and to aiding the victims, both primary and secondary, of False Memory Syndrome.

### GriefNet

http://www.griefnet.org

Bereavement, grief, death and dying resources.

### Institute of Psychiatry Library: Mental Health

http://www.iop.kcl.ac.uk/IoP/AdminSup/Library/psy/ment.stm

A very comprehensive list of links to resources in mental health.

### The International Society for Mental Health Online

http://www.ismho.org/

The International Society for Mental Health Online (ISMHO) was formed in 1997 to promote the understanding, use and development of online communication, information and technology for the international mental health community.

### Knowledge Exchange Network

http://www.mentalhealth.org/

KEN—the National Mental Health Services Knowledge Exchange Network—has an award-winning Web site that offers a wealth of information about mental health. Visitors can find a variety of mental health-related subjects from advocacy to Zoloft™, alternative care to managed care, anxiety disorders to statistics.

### Louis de la Parte Florida Mental Health Institute

http://www.fmhi.usf.edu/

The state's primary research and training center for mental health services is recognized nationally for its innovative research and training. The site offers information about mental health needs and services in the state of Florida, and links to relevant information, including electronic publications.

### Mental Health Matters!

http://www.mental-health-matters.com/

Mental Health Matters! is a directory of mental health and mental illness information, and resources for mental health professionals, patients, and families.

### Mental Health Net

http://mentalhclp.net/

MHN considers itself the largest, most comprehensive guide to mental health online, featuring over 7,000 individual resources. This site, winner of several awards, covers information on disorders such as depression, anxiety, panic attacks, chronic fatigue syndrome and substance abuse, to professional resources in psychology, psychiatry and social work, journals, and self-help magazines.

### The Mining Company Mental Health Resources

http://mentalhealth.miningco.com/

The Mining Company (a part of about.com) has developed more than 700 World Wide Web guides in a variety of topical areas. The Mental Health guide was developed by Leonard Holmes, a clinical psychologist in private practice who also provides mental health services over the Net. The site provides links to an impressive variety of informational resources for mental health.

### National Alliance for the Mentally Ill

http://www.nami.org/

Grassroots, self-help organization of people with serious mental illness and their families and friends. NAMI's mission is to eradicate mental illness and to improve the quality of life for those who have mental illness.

### National Center for PTSD

http://www.ncptsd.org/

U.S. Department of Veterans Affairs National Center for PTSD offers research and education on Post-Traumatic Stress Disorder.

### National Institute of Mental Health

http://www.nimh.nih.gov/

General information about NIMH, public information about mental health, including videos, news and announcements from NIMH, grants, contracts, and committee information, and information on NIMH research activities.

### National Mental Health Association

`http://www.nmha.org/`

The National Mental Health Association, through its national office and more than 300 affiliates nationwide, is dedicated to improving the mental health of all individuals and achieving victory over mental illnesses.

### Post Traumatic Stress Disorder Links

`http://www.lawandpsychiatry.com/html/ptsdlinks.htm`

A list of excellent links from Mark Levy, MD, who specializes in forensic psychiatry.

### Psychiatry Online

`http://www.priory.co.uk/psych.htm`

The International Forum for Psychiatry—a peer reviewed, independent psychiatry journal for psychiatrists and mental health professionals. Contains articles, archives, and links to professional resources.

### Specifica Mental Health Resources

`http://www.realtime.net/~mmjw/`

A topical list of references for consumers by Jeanine Wade, Ph.D.

### Stress Free NET

`http://www.stressfree.com/`

StressFree Net offers stress related services and tools, including a directory of health and stress management professionals to help the user, and an opportunity to "Ask the Psychologist."

### Screening for Suicide Risk

`http://cpmcnet.columbia.edu/texts/gcps/gcps0060.html`

Important information on screening for suicide intent from Columbia-Presbyterian Medical Center.

### Therapist Referral Network

`http://fmpweb-store.com/trn`

*Research Navigator Guide: Helping Professions*

TRN is a free service providing users with information to help them search for licensed psychotherapists and other mental health services. The program allows a detailed search for licensed professionals by location based on specialization, fee, insurance plan, theoretical orientation, and more.

### UCLA School Mental Health Project

http://smhp.psych.ucla.edu/

The School Mental Health Project (SMHP) was created to pursue theory, research, practice and training related to meeting the mental health needs of youngsters through school-based interventions. Their award winning Web site offers information on our clearinghouse, introductory packets, consultation cadre, newsletter, links to other Internet sites and electronic networking.

### The Wounded Healer Journal

http://twhj.com/

Issues of grief and loss for survivors of sexual abuse.

## POLICY PRACTICE

### NOW and Welfare

http://now.org/issues/economic/welfare/

The National Organization for Women presents a policy analysis relating welfare reform and domestic violence.

### Behaviorists for Social Responsibility

http://www.bfsr.org/

BFSR is a Special Interest Group of the Association for Behavior Analysis. The SIG and the site are dedicated to applications of the science of behavior and cultural analysis to issues of social importance, including education, human rights, environmental, and social justice issues. The site includes links to related state-of-the art publications and related sites.

### Canadian Centre for Policy Alternatives

http://www.policyalternatives.ca/

The Canadian Centre for Policy Alternatives was founded in 1980 to promote research on economic and social issues facing Canada. The Centre monitors current developments in the economy and studies important trends that affect Canadians. The Web site provides information about the activities of the center, its publications and links to related resources.

### Canadian Council on Social Development

http://www.ccsd.ca/

The Canadian Council on Social Development is a voluntary, nonprofit organization whose mission is to develop and promote progressive social policies inspired by social justice, equality and the empowerment of individuals and communities through research, consultation, public education and advocacy. The Web site features information about the center and access to its statistical databases.

### Centre for Social Policy Research and Development

http://www.bangor.ac.uk/csprd/

The Centre for Social Policy Research and Development (CSPRD) at the University of Wales, Bangor, is committed to the conduct of well-founded, scientific research primarily in the areas of human development, health studies and social care provision. The site offers information about the center, research reports, and links to related resources.

### The Century Foundation

http://www.tcf.org/

This site is designed to substitute facts for myth in the important public battle over welfare reform. The Century Foundation is a nonprofit, nonpartisan foundation that sponsors and supervises research on economic, social, and political issues. Contributors to the information presented on the site include Joel Handler, Professor of Law, University of California, Los Angeles; Yeheskel Hasenfeld, Professor of Social Welfare, University of California, Los Angeles; and Jack Sirica of *Newsday*.

### Congress Merge

http://www.congressmerge.com/

Congress Merge uses technology to assist legislative/congressional lobbying and advocacy efforts. Congress Merge provides tables linking zip codes to congressional and/or state legislative districts as well as tables with legislator contact information, committee assignments, biographies and district offices.

### Congress.org—A Guide to the U.S. Congress

http://congress.org/

Congress.org is an updated online directory of information for both the US House of Representatives and the US Senate. A comprehensive resource for communicating with Congress, the structure and features of Congress.org can be customized to the needs of any organization or business involved in public affairs or grassroots activities.

### Contacting the Congress

http://www.visi.com/juan/congress/

Contacting the Congress is a very up-to-date database of congressional contact information for the 107th Congress. As of July 11, 2001 there are 510 email addresses (of which 202 are Web-based email home pages), and 536 WWW home pages known for the 540 members of the 107th Congress. More traditional ground mail addresses are available for all Congress members.

### The Electronic Activist

http://gemini.berkshire.net/~ifas/activist/

An email address directory of congress people, state governments, and media, from the Institute for First Amendment Studies.

### Electronic Policy Network

http://epn.org/

EPN considers itself to be the clearinghouse for the latest progressive policy research and reports from the nation's leading research institutes, think tanks, and policy organizations. The site provides online compendia of news and individual policy issues, a search engine, access to a mailing list to keep up with policy developments as they happen, and topical links to member institutions and beyond.

### Federal News Service

http://www.fnsg.com/

FNS allows you to read the actual words spoken by national leaders on matters of official U.S. Government policy and other issues of the day, the same day.

### The Lindesmith Center—Drug Policy Foundation

http://www.lindesmith.org/

The Lindesmith Center—Drug Policy Foundation is a drug policy organization working to broaden and better inform the public debate on drug policy and related issues. The Lindesmith Center, created in 1994, is the leading independent drug policy institute in the United States.

### MIMH/PIE Confluence Page

http://pie.org/

A joint project of the Missouri Institute of Mental Health and the Policy Information Exchange, this is a comprehensive mental health policy Internet resource. The MIMH side of the site provides information about the activities of the center, which is housed at the University of Missouri–Columbia. It also provides links to related sites, consumer information, and access to its publications. PIE Online is one of the largest online collections of health and mental health policy information available anywhere. Textual and statistical information, documents, bibliographies, reviews, federal and state legislative information, job and funding opportunities, and events calendars can be found quickly using PIE Online's full text retrieval capabilities. PIE is available by subscription only, which may be the way of the future on the Internet.

### PoliticsOnline

http://www.politicsonline.com/

This site is devoted to providing tools, tips and news about how to use the Internet to make political communications more effective.

### PRAXIS

http://www.ssw.upenn.edu/~restes/praxis.html

The international development home page of Prof. Richard J. Estes of the University of Pennsylvania, this site to an array of archival resources on international and comparative social development designed to meet the informational needs of social work educators and students with international interests and other educators and students who require assistance in locating useful national and international resources on social and economic development.

### Project Vote Smart

http://www.vote-smart.org/

Project Vote Smart tracks the performance of over 13,000 political leaders, including the President, Congress, Governors, and State Legislatures.

### United Nations Development Program

http://www.undp.org/

UNDP's overarching mission is to help countries build national capacity to achieve sustainable, human development, giving top priority to eliminating poverty and building equity.

### The University of Michigan Gerald R. Ford School of Public Policy

http://www.spp.umich.edu/

Formerly the Institute for Public Policy Studies, the Gerald R. Ford School of Public Policy became an independent school within the University of Michigan in 1995. In addition to providing information about the programs offered by the School of Public Policy, the site also provides a working paper archive.

### Welfare Policy Center

http://www.hudson.org/wpc/

The Welfare Policy Center (WPC) conducts research and provides technical assistance on welfare reform and related issues. It is a resource for policymakers, program administrators, the press, and many others seeking to learn about cutting-edge welfare reforms and what it takes to make reforms effective. This Web site provides information about key welfare issues and interesting welfare-related articles.

### The Welfare to Work Partnership

http://www.welfaretowork.org/

The Welfare to Work Partnership is a nonpartisan, nonprofit organization created by the American business community to provide innovative workforce solutions for companies through hiring, retaining and promoting welfare recipients and other unemployed and low-income workers.

### Western New York Law Center

http://www.wnylc.net

The Western New York Law Center maintains the Welfare Law Area resource, designed to assist welfare advocates with helpful information.

## PREVENTION

### Child Abuse Prevention Network

http://child-abuse.com/

Originally developed through an initiative of Family Life Development Center at Cornell University, the network is dedicated to enhancing Internet resources for the prevention of child abuse and neglect, and reducing the negative conditions in the family and the community that lead to child maltreatment.

### Committee for Children

http://www.cfchildren.org/

Committee for Children provides classroom curricula for the prevention of child abuse and youth violence as well as training and parent education. They also conduct original research evaluating the effectiveness of their programs.

### Community Psychology Network

http://www.cmmtypsych.net/

Community Psychology Net is the Web's most comprehensive site dedicated to the field of community psychology. This site is meant to be a resource for educators, professionals, researchers, graduate and undergraduate students, and others who are interested in learning more about the fascinating field of community psychology, action research, intervention, and prevention. The site provides links to discussion lists, professional membership groups, graduate schools, course materials, funding sources, position announcements, social policy information, and various other miscellaneous resources relevant to the field.

### Let's Prevent Abuse

http://www.pacer.org/app/lpa.htm

This Minneapolis-based program provides resources to families and professionals for the prevention of child abuse with a focus on disability and cultural competency.

### National Clearinghouse on Child Abuse and Neglect Information

http://www.calib.com/nccanch/

Supported by the Children's Bureau, The National Clearinghouse on Child Abuse and Neglect Information is a national resource for professionals seeking information on the prevention, identification, and treatment of child abuse and neglect, and related child welfare issues.

### National Drug Prevention League

http://www.ndpl.org/

The NDPL is an association of over 25 national and major regional private sector organizations for drug abuse prevention. The site provides links to related resources and information, including national surveys and studies, federal programs and budgets and congressional bills.

*Research Navigator Guide: Helping Professions*

### Oregon Social Learning Center

http://www.oslc.org/

Providing information, educational experiences, and networking opportunities for researchers, interventionists, and advocates dedicated to the science of prevention.

### Parents Anonymous

http://www.parentsanonymous-natl.org/

Parents Anonymous is the nation's oldest and largest child abuse prevention organization dedicated to strengthening families through innovative strategies that promote mutual support and parent leadership.

### Partnership for a Drug-Free America

http://www.drugfreeamerica.org/

This site includes a comprehensive database of drug information: what they do, what they look like, their history, and slang terms.

## RESEARCH AND MEASUREMENT

### The Action Evaluation Project

http://www.ARIAssociates.haverford.edu/

The ARIA Group is a conflict-resolution consulting firm based in Yellow Springs, Ohio with Associates around the world. It assists organizational and community leaders to creatively transform deep and destructive conflict. The ARIA Group is associated with The Action Evaluation Project, which has developed a new methodology for participatory and empowering evaluation. The site is dedicated to demonstrating this new evaluation methodology.

### Alcoholism Treatment Assessment Instruments

http://www.niaaa.nih.gov/publications/instable.htm

Information on the availability of a variety of instruments for adolescents and adults to be used in screening, diagnosis, assessment of drinking behavior, treatment planning, treatment and process assessment, and outcome evaluation.

### AlphaLogic

http://www.pdq4.com/

Presents the Personality Diagnostic Questionnaire (PDQ-4), a user-friendly interactive program that determines the presence of personality disorders consistent with the DSM-IV, Axis II.

### American Evaluation Association

http://www.eval.org/

An international professional association of evaluators devoted to the application and exploration of program evaluation, personnel evaluation, technology, and other forms of evaluation.

### American FactFinder

http://factfinder.census.gov/

In 1996, the US Census undertook a comprehensive multi-year development effort to build a data dissemination system. American FactFinder uses high performance computing systems to enable users to select data tabulations and maps from data sets in the system.

### American Institutes for Research

http://www.air-dc.org/

AIR is an independent, not-for-profit corporation that performs basic and applied research, provides technical support, and conducts analyses in the behavioral and social sciences.

### American Psychological Association Science Directorate: Testing and Assessment

http://www.apa.org/science/testing.html

American Psychological Association provides answers to Frequently Asked Questions about the selection and use of psychological tests.

### American Sociological Association Section on Methods

http://www.icpsr.umich.edu/methsect/

Provides information about the activities of the section.

### ANU—Coombsweb

http://coombs.anu.edu.au/

This archive site was established to act as an electronic repository of the social science and humanities papers, bibliographies, directories, theses abstracts and other high-grade research material produced (or deposited) at the Research Schools of Social Sciences and Pacific and Asian Studies, Australian National University, Canberra, Australia.

### Bioethics Resources on the Web

http://www.nih.gov/sigs/bioethics/IRB.html

An excellent list of resources about human subjects research and Institutional Review Boards from the National Institutes for Health.

### Bureau of Justice Assistance Evaluation Web Site

http://www.bja.evaluationwebsite.org/

The Bureau of Justice Assistance is committed to the importance of program evaluation and to developing and enhancing evaluation capabilities at State and local levels. This Web site is designed to provide State Administrative Agency staff, criminal justice planners, researchers and evaluators, as well as local practitioners with a variety of resources for evaluating criminal justice programs.

### Buros Institute of Mental Measurements

http://www.unl.edu/buros/

Comprehensive site providing reviews of tests, links to important resources for testing, and standards for utilization of tests.

### Center for Demography and Ecology

http://www.ssc.wisc.edu/cde/

CDE is a multi-disciplinary faculty research cooperative for social scientific demographic research whose membership includes sociologists, rural sociologists, economists, and historians.

### Center for Social Research Methods

http://trochim.human.cornell.edu/

This Web site, developed by Bill Trochim at Cornell, is intended for people involved in applied social research and evaluation. There are many links to other locations on the Web that deal in applied social research methods, previously published and unpublished papers, detailed examples of current research projects, useful tools for researchers (like a guide to selecting a statistical analysis), an extensive online textbook, a bulletin board for discussions, and more.

### Cochrane Collaboration

http://hiru.mcmaster.ca/cochrane/

Facilitates the creative, review, maintenance and dissemination of systematic overviews of the effects of health care.

### Community of Science

http://www.cos.com/

The mission of the Community of Science (COS) is to provide rapid, easy-to-use information about scientists and the funding of science. The Community of Science is a global registry designed to provide accurate, timely, easy-to-access information about what new funding opportunities exist, and who is working on what subject, and where.

### Content Analysis Resources

http://www.gsu.edu/~wwwcom/

Resources to assist researchers utilizing content analysis strategies, including reviews of publications, bibliographies, and software.

### Corporate Grantmakers on the Internet

http://fdncenter.org/funders/grantmaker/gws_corp/corp2.html

Annotated listing of interests and geographic limitations of scores of company-sponsored private foundations and direct corporate giving programs.

### CSAC Ethnographics Gallery Software Archives

http://lucy.ukc.ac.uk/archives.html

Shareware statistics program, SchoolStat™. Graphic display of probability distributions, spread sheet, and a variety of parametric and nonparametric statistics.

### ERIC Clearinghouse on Assessment and Evaluation

http://www.ericae.net/

Information pertaining to educational and psychological testing and learning theories. Provides balanced information concerning educational assessment and resources to encourage responsible test use.

### Funding Institutions—Foundations

http://resource.ca.jhu.edu/foundations.html

A listing of foundations from Johns Hopkins University.

### Geriatric Depression Scale

http://www.vh.org/Providers/ClinRef/FPHandbook/
Chapter15/01-15.html#Box 15-2

Scale measuring depression in elderly subjects.

### Glossary of Selected Social Science Computing and Social Science Terms

http://odwin.ucsd.edu/glossary/

Covers terms that may be useful in managing data collections and providing basic data services.

### Idea Works, Inc.

http://www.ideaworks.com/

An information technology company specializing in the development and publication of expert systems for business, industry, research, and human services. Services include training, consulting, development, publication, and contract services.

### The Illinois Researcher Information Service (IRIS)

http://www.library.uiuc.edu/iris/

The Illinois Researcher Information Service (IRIS) is a unit of the University of Illinois Library at Urbana-Champaign. The IRIS office compiles the IRIS database of funding opportunities. The office also maintains a library of publications (informational brochures, application guidelines, and annual reports) from over 2,000 funding agencies.

### Institute for the Advancement of Social Work Research

http://www.cosw.sc.edu/iaswr/

IASWR was founded in 1993 by five national professional organizations that represent the social work practice and education communities. In 2000, a new social work research organization became a sponsor. A freestanding, not-for-profit organization, IASWR serves the research needs of the entire social work profession. Sponsoring organizations are represented on the Board of Directors of IASWR and contribute annually to its financial support. IASWR promotes social work research conducted under the auspices of other academic and professional organizations. IASWR does not conduct or fund social work research directly, except in surveys on behalf of the profession which relate to fulfilling Institute goals.

Research Navigator Guide: Helping Professions

### Institute for Social Research

http://www.isr.umich.edu/

Information about the research facility at the University of Michigan. Includes the Survey Research Center, the Research Center for Group Dynamics, and the Center for Political Studies.

### Internal Validity Tutorial

http://psych.athabascau.ca/html/Validity/

This self-instructional tutorial on internal validity that teaches students to recognize and analyze flaws in the design of clinical experiments.

### International Index of Social Progress

http://www.globalideasbank.org/BOV/BV-377.HTML

Measures economic development, social and political conditions, and the ability of nations to produce welfare services for their citizens.

### Internet Resources for Institutional Research

http://airweb.org/links/

Links to assist institutional researchers and faculty and students in higher education in navigating the Internet.

### Methods Resources

http://research.ed.asu.edu/

Research methods resources from the College of Education at Arizona State University.

### National Institutes of Health Funding Opportunities

http://grants.nih.gov/grants/

Information about NIH grant and fellowship programs, applying for a grant or fellowship, policy changes, administrative responsibilities of awardees, the CRISP database, and the numbers and characteristics of awards made by the NIH.

### On Being a Scientist: Responsible Conduct in Research

http://www.nap.edu/readingroom/books/obas/

An online publication of the Committee on Science, Engineering, and Public Policy of the National Academy of Sciences.

### OpinionMeter

http://www.opinionmeter.com/

Interactive fully-automated polling machine to measure customer satisfaction.

### Power Analysis

http://hedwig.mgh.harvard.edu/size.html

Statistical considerations for determining sample size, power, and the minimal detectable difference in clinical trials and scientific experiments.

### Power Calculator

http://ebook.stat.ucla.edu/calculators/powercalc/

Web-based software to determine statistical power.

### Private Foundations on the Internet

http://fdncenter.org/funders/grantmaker/
gws_priv/priv2.html

Annotated listing detailing interests and geographical limitations of hundreds of private foundations.

### ProGAMMA: Social Science Information Technology

http://www.gamma.rug.nl/

Information Technology for the Social and Behavioral sciences (SSIT)

### Psychological Maltreatment of Women Inventory

http://www.umich.edu/~rtolman/pmwimas.htm

Created by Richard Tolman at University of Michigan to investigate woman abuse.

### Qualitative Methods (QualPage)

http://www.ualberta.ca/~jrnorris/qual.html

Resources for qualitative researchers.

### RAND

http://www.rand.org/

Through research and analysis, RAND assists public policymakers at all levels, private sector leaders in many industries, and the public at large in efforts to strengthen the nation's economy, maintain its security, and improve its quality of life.

### REGARD

http://www.regard.ac.uk/

REGARD is a searchable bibliographic database containing in-depth information on UK social science research. It is wholly funded by the Economic and Social Research Council (ESRC) with hardware support from Sun Microsystems.

### Research for a New Age

http://www.nia.nih.gov/health/pubs/research

Discusses various aspects of databased decision making for care decisions with geriatric patients.

### Russell Sage Foundation

http://www.russellsage.org/

The principal American foundation devoted exclusively to research in the social sciences, the Foundation is a research center, a funding source for studies by scholars at other academic and research institutions, and an active member of the nation's social science community.

### Social Science Information Gateway (SOSIG)

http://sosig.esrc.bris.ac.uk/

The Social Science Information Gateway (SOSIG) aims to provide a trusted source of selected, high quality Internet information for researchers and practitioners in the social sciences, business and law. It is part of the UK Resource Discovery Network.

### Social Science Research Center

http://www.ssrc.msstate.edu/

The SSRC at Mississippi State University makes available many of their research reports on this site.

### Society for Judgment and Decision-Making

http://www.sjdm.org/

The Society for Judgment and Decision Making is an interdisciplinary organization dedicated to the study of normative, descriptive, and prescriptive theories of decision.

### StatCenter

`http://www.utah.edu/stat/`

StatCenter is a set of diverse resources for teaching and learning introductory statistics over the web. It is not a stand-alone course that teaches statistics and delivers credit. It is meant to support teachers and students with already-existing classes.

### StatLib

`http://www.stat.cmu.edu/`

StatLib is a system for distributing statistical software, datasets, and information by email, FTP, and WWW. It is a service of the Carnegie Mellon University Statistics Department.

### Statistical Resources on the Internet

`http://www.stat.vt.edu/links.htm`

It is provided as a starting point for locating statistics-related information on the World Wide Web.

### Statistical Software Support

`http://www.aom.pace.edu/rmd/statsoft.html`

Part of the Research Methods Web site at the Academy of Management.

### The Statistics Home Page

`http://www.statsoftinc.com/textbook/stathome.html`

This Electronic Statistical Textbook offers training in the understanding and application of statistics. The material was developed based on many years of teaching undergraduate and graduate statistics courses and covers a wide variety of applications, including laboratory research, business statistics and forecasting, social science statistics and survey research, data mining, engineering and quality control applications.

### Substance Abuse Subtle Screening Inventory

`http://www.cerainc.com/html/sas.html`

Substance abuse screening from Consultation, Education, and Research Associates.

### University Center for Urban and Social Research

`http://www.ucsur.pitt.edu/`

Established at University of Pittsburgh to carry out basic and applied social science research, the UCSUR is a focal point for collaborative interdisciplinary and multidisciplinary approaches to social science and policy issues.

### Web Resources for Educational Research and Evaluation

`http://www.stanford.edu/~davidf/class/`
`webresources.htm`

An excellent set of links, most of which are equally applicable to social work research and evaluation, maintained by David Fetterman.

### The World Wide Web Virtual Library: Statistics

`http://www.stat.ufl.edu/vlib/statistics.html`

A cornucopia of links related to statistics.

## SEXUALITY

### Coalition for Positive Sexuality

`http://www.positive.org/`

The Coalition for Positive Sexuality was formed to give teens the information about sexuality they need to take care of themselves and affirm their decisions about sex, sexuality, and reproductive control. They also hope to facilitate dialogue, in and out of the public schools, on condom availability and sex education. Just Say Yes, their irreverent and unabashed comprehensive sex education guide is available here.

### Collected Domestic Partner Information

`http://www.cs.cmu.edu/afs/cs/user/scotts/`
`domestic-partners/`

A collection of information about the issues of domestic partner policies, same sex marriages, and adoption.

### The Data Lounge: Lesbian/Gay Internet

`http://www.datalounge.com/`

Daily News, Culture and Gossip, Forums and Weekly Surveys. Global Lesbian/Gay Calendar. Web Directory and Edwina's Dating Service.

*Research Navigator Guide: Helping Professions*

### Deaf Queer Resource Center

`http://www.deafqueer.org/`

DQRC is a national nonprofit information center. Considered to be "the place" to find comprehensive and accurate information about the deaf queer community.

### Gay Canada

`http://www.cglbrd.com/`

The first GLB community based information network for Canadian gays, lesbians, and bisexuals, this site contains a impressive set of resources, updated frequently.

### The Gay Connection

`http://www.thegayconnection.com/`

A gay, lesbian, bisexual one-stop resource site.

### !OutProud!

`http://www.outproud.org/`

This the WWW site for the National Coalition for Gay, Lesbian, and Bisexual Youth. The site offers a wide range of resources for youth and educators.

### Queer Frontiers

`http://www.usc.edu/isd/archives/queerfrontiers/queer/beyond/`

1995 Conference Proceedings and Beyond: A Scholarly Resource for Queer Theory and Studies. The focus of ongoing content development for "Beyond 1995" is on a queer theoretically focused investigation, analysis and critique of the Internet's cultural and social significance and impact and how it is itself generating a whole new cyber-culture and subsequent cyber-reality.

### Qworld

`http://www.qworld.com`

Qworld, a "web location for queer information, news, and community," is a fun and informational site hosting two online magazines, chat areas and message boards, a listing of gay-friendly professionals, regional resources, and the Qfiles, which offer everything from health information to shareware.

### Steven Capsuto's Home Page

http://www.stevecap.com/

Through his Links-o-Rama, an extensive listing of resources for gay men and lesbians, bisexual men and women, and transgendered individuals.

### Transgender Forum

http://www.tgfmall.com/

A resource guide for crossdressers, transvestites, transsexuals, transgendered people, their family and friends.

### Youth Assistance Organization/Youth Action Online

http://youth.org/

This is a service run by volunteers, created to help self-identifying gay, lesbian, bisexual and questioning youth. YAO exists to provide young people with a safe space online to be themselves. The site offers information for youths questioning their sexuality, an online magazine, and links to other resources on the Internet.

## SUBSTANCE ABUSE

### Alcoholics Anonymous

http://www.alcoholics-anonymous.org/

Information about the self-help organization.

### AL-ANON and ALATEEN

http://www.Al-Anon-Alateen.org/

These are worldwide organizations that offer self-help recovery programs for families and friends of alcoholics whether or not the alcoholic seeks help or even recognizes the existence of a drinking problem.

### American Society of Addiction Medicine

http://www.asam.org/

The medical specialty society dedicated to educating physicians and improving the treatment of individuals suffering from alcoholism or other addictions.

### AMERSA

http://www.amersa.org/

Association for Medical Education and Research in Substance Abuse, sponsored by the Center for Alcohol and Addiction Studies at Brown University.

### APA Division 28

http://www.apa.org/divisions/div28/

American Psychological Association Division 28 is the special interest group for psychopharmacology and Substance Abuse. This page offers their archives and information on research opportunities.

### Canadian Centre on Substance Abuse

http://www.ccsa.ca/

A nonprofit organization working to minimize the harm associated with the use of alcohol, tobacco and other drugs, this site offers links to a wealth of resources, including online courses on substance abuse topics.

### Center for Alcohol and Addiction Studies

http://center.butler.brown.edu/

Features information about the work of the Brown University center and links to related resources.

### Center for Education and Drug Abuse Research

http://cedar.pharmacy.pitt.edu/

Information on CEDAR, an ongoing 20-year prospective family/high-risk study of substance abuse, including grant information, description of the design and research modules, list of publications, news, and links to other drug-related resources.

### Center for Substance Abuse Prevention

http://www.samhsa.gov/centers/csap/csap.html

CSAP Technical Assistance Services to Communities is a unique federally funded program designed to disseminate information, increase dialog, and promote community empowerment to combat alcohol and other drug problems.

### Centre for Addiction and Mental Health

`http://www.camh.net/`

The Centre for Addiction and Mental Health is a public hospital providing direct patient care for people with mental health and addiction problems. The Centre was created in 1998 through the successful merger of the Clarke Institute of Psychiatry, the Addiction Research Foundation, the Queen Street Mental Health Centre and the Donwood Institute. The Addiction Research Foundation, founded in 1949, was one of North America's pre-eminent facilities for research into alcohol, tobacco and other drug problems. The Foundation's current mission is to work with its partners to create and apply knowledge to prevent and reduce substance abuse in Ontario. The CAMH collaborates with the World Health Organization, participating in international research and carrying out training programs in other countries.

### Cocaine Anonymous

`http://www.ca.org/`

Cocaine Anonymous is a 12-step fellowship of men and women who share their experience, strength and hope with each other so that they may solve their common problem and help others to recover from their addiction.

### Dual Diagnosis Web Site

`http://www.erols.com/ksciacca/`

Dual Diagnosis refers to co-occurring Mental Illness, Drug Addiction and/or Alcoholism in various combinations. This site is designed to provide information and resources for service providers, consumers, and family members who are seeking assistance and/or education in this field.

### LifeRing Secular Recovery

`http://www.unhooked.com/`

LifeRing is an alternative recovery method for those alcoholics or drug addicts who are uncomfortable with the spiritual content of widely available 12-Step programs.

### Narcotics Anonymous

`http://na.org/`

Narcotics Anonymous is an international, community-based association of recovering drug addicts. Started in 1947, the NA movement is one of the world's oldest and largest of its type, with nearly twenty thousand weekly meetings in seventy countries.

### National Alliance of Methadone Advocates

http://www.methadone.org/

NAMA is an organization composed of methadone maintenance patients and supporters of quality methadone maintenance treatment.

### National Association of Alcoholism and Drug Abuse Counselors

http://www.naadac.org/

NAADAC's mission is to provide leadership in the alcoholism and drug abuse counseling profession. The site offers information about the organization and links to important resources.

### National Organization on Fetal Alcohol Syndrome

http://www.nofas.org/

NOFAS is a nonprofit organization dedicated to eliminating birth defects caused by alcohol consumption during pregnancy and improving the quality of life for those individuals and families affected. NOFAS is the only national organization focusing solely on FAS, the leading known cause of mental retardation.

### Arizona Smokers Helpline

http://www.ashline.org

This site is sponsored by the Arizona Program for Nicotine and Tobacco Research at the University of Arizona. This page is a great place to visit to find resources on quitting and for general information about quitting smoking.

### Prevline: National Clearinghouse for Alcohol and Drug Information

http://www.health.org/

Offers electronic access to searchable databases and substance abuse prevention materials that pertain to alcohol, tobacco, and drugs.

### The Research Institute on Addictions

http://www.ria.org/

RIA in Buffalo, New York, is a national leader in alcohol and substance abuse prevention, treatment, and policy research. The site offers information about the work of the center, including its Minority Research Development Program.

### Sobriety and Recovery Resources

http://www.recoveryresources.org/

Links to personal testimonials and information about self-help, largely 12-step, groups.

### Society for Research on Nicotine and Tobacco

http://www.srnt.org/

SRNT is composed of over 500 of the world's leading scientists in tobacco and nicotine research. The mission of the Society is to stimulate the generation of new knowledge concerning nicotine in all its manifestations—from molecular to societal. The site provides links to research resources, training and research opportunities, and other resources.

### Substance Abuse and Mental Health Services Administration

http://www.samhsa.gov/

The SAMHSA home page offers links to a wide variety of resources.

### Web of Addictions

http://www.well.com/user/woa/

The Web of Addictions is dedicated to providing accurate information about alcohol and other drug addictions and a resource for teachers, students and others who need factual information about abused drugs.

## VIOLENCE

### Act Against Violence Outreach Campaign

http://idahoptv.org/outreach/acts/

Act Against Violence is a multi-year, solutions-based public television outreach effort which combines programming, print materials, and community events to help reduce youth violence.

### Bureau of Justice Statistics Crime and Victims Statistics

http://www.ojp.usdoj.gov/bjs/cvict.htm

Information, statistics, and publications about criminal victimization in the United States and related data collections.

### Center for the Study and Prevention of Violence

http://www.colorado.edu/cspv/

The Center for the Study and Prevention of Violence (CSPV) was founded in 1992 with a grant from the Carnegie Corporation of New York to provide informed assistance to groups committed to understanding and preventing violence, particularly adolescent violence.

### Child Abuse Prevention Network

http://child-abuse.com/

This site is dedicated to using the World Wide Web to give child abuse prevention professionals the fullest possible support in their work. A seemingly inexhaustible reference of links for professionals.

### Community United Against Violence

http://www.xq.com/cuav/

CUAV is a 15-year-old nonprofit agency that addresses and prevents hate violence directed at lesbians, gay men, bisexuals, and transgendered persons.

### Domestic Violence Handbook

http://www.domesticviolence.org/

This online resource is designed to assist women who are experiencing domestic abuse.

### Domestic Violence Hotlines

http://www.feminist.org/911/crisis.html

Links to telephone, postal, and electronic addresses for domestic violence hotlines across the country.

### The Family Peace Project

http://www.family.mcw.edu/FamilyPeaceProject.htm

The Family Peace Project provides education, training and consultation to citizens, health care professionals, organizations and communities. Staff for the Project consists of psychologists and community activists who believe that citizens can improve their communities by using the power of individual responsibility, civic action and the democratic process to engage the strengths and resources of our local communities and create local solutions.

### Family Violence Prevention Fund

`http://endabuse.org`

Endabuse is a national nonprofit organization that focuses on domestic violence education, prevention and public policy reform. The site provides a host of links to domestic violence sites, allied organizations, and other resources.

### Guggenheim Foundation Research on Violence and Aggression

`http://www.hfg.org/`

The Harry Frank Guggenheim Foundation sponsors scholarly research on problems of violence, aggression, and dominance. The foundation provides both research grants to established scholars and dissertation fellowships to graduate students during the dissertation-writing year. The *HFG Review* of research is published on a semi-annual basis.

### GUNFREE

`http://www.gunfree.org/`

The Coalition to Stop Gun Violence was founded to combat the growing gun violence problem in the United States. CSGV is a unique coalition of more than forty religious, professional, labor, medical, educational and civic organizations.

### The Harvard Youth Violence Prevention Center

`http://www.hsph.harvard.edu/php/VPP/hyvpc.html`

The Harvard Youth Violence Prevention Center (HYVPC) is an innovative, multi-disciplinary center based at the Harvard School of Public Health. The Center's theme is "Research Partnerships with Communities." Center activities are based upon the premise that effective prevention evolves from mutually respectful, reciprocal relationships between researchers, community members, and policy makers.

### Justice Information Center (NCJRS): Victims Domestic and Family Violence

`http://www.ncjrs.org/victdv.htm`

Links to documents about domestic and family violence.

### Mapping Policies and Actions

`http://www.harbour.sfu.ca/freda/reports/pol.htm`

This site presents an annotated bibliography about violence against women. The material in this bibliography is organized into subject areas. The broad subject areas include; criminal justice, civil/family law, health, economic/social welfare, housing, education/curriculum, community-based programs and services and literature reviews.

### Minnesota Higher Education Center Against Violence and Abuse

http://www.mincava.umn.edu/

The goal of the Clearinghouse is to provide a quick and user-friendly access point to the extensive electronic resources on the topic of violence and abuse available through the Internet. It offers access to thousands of Gopher servers, interactive discussion groups, newsgroups and Web sites around the world.

### The National Center for Victims of Crime

http://www.ncvc.org/

The National Center for Victims of Crime provides assistance to victims of crime and providers of assistance to victims of crime.

### National Coalition Against Domestic Violence

http://www.webmerchants.com/ncadv/

NCADV is a grassroots nonprofit membership organization working since 1978 to end violence in the lives of women and children. They provide a national network for state coalitions and local programs serving battered women and their children, public policy at the national level, technical assistance, community awareness campaigns, general information and referrals, and publications on the issue of domestic violence, sponsor of a national conference every two years for battered women and their advocates.

### National Consortium on Violence Research

http://www.ncovr.org/

NCOVR has been created as a research and training center devoted to studying the factors contributing to inter-personal violence. The NCOVR World Wide Web site is served by the H. John Heinz III School of Public Policy and Management at Carnegie Mellon University in Pittsburgh, Pennsylvania.

### National Network of Violence Prevention Practitioners

http://www2.edc.org/nvpp/

The NNVPP specializes in the preparation and distribution of curricula that synthesize violence prevention information, as well as providing specialized training and technical assistance to practitioners nationwide.

### NOW and Violence Against Women

http://now.org/issues/violence

Information from the National Organization for Women about violence against women.

### Pacific Center for Violence Prevention

http://www.pcvp.org/

The Pacific Center for Violence Prevention, a project of the Trauma Foundation, works to prevent youth violence in California. Located at San Francisco General Hospital, the Center serves as the policy headquarters for the Violence Prevention Initiative funded by The California Wellness Foundation.

### Partnerships Against Violence Network

http://pavnet.org/

PAVNET Online is a "virtual library" of information about violence and youth-at-risk, representing data from seven different federal agencies. It considers itself a "one-stop", searchable, information resource to help reduce redundancy in information management and provide clear and comprehensive access to information for states and local communities.

### Rape, Abuse, and Incest National Network

http://www.rainn.org/

RAINN is a nonprofit organization based in Washington, D.C. that operates a national toll-free hotline for victims of sexual assault.

### SafetyNet Domestic Violence Resources

http://www.cybergrrl.com/views/dv/

A compendium of a wide range of information related to the issue of domestic violence.

### The Silent Witness National Initiative

http://www.silentwitness.net/

In 1990, an ad hoc group of women artists and writers, upset about the growing number of women in Minnesota being murdered by their partners or acquaintances, joined together with several other women's organizations to form Arts Action Against Domestic Violence, which has as its goal the promotion of successful community-based domestic violence reduction efforts in order to reach zero domestic murders by 2010.

### Violence Against Women and Sexual Harassment

`http://www.feminist.com/violence/`

Anti-Violence Resources at Feminist.com.

### Violence and Abuse in Couples Project

`http://www.ackerman.org/violence.htm`

This project has as its goal the development of a feminist-informed, morally explicit systemic conjoint treatment model to end violence by men toward their female partners.

### Women, Co-Occurring Disorders & Violence Study

`http://www.prainc.com/wcdvs/`

The Center for Substance Abuse Treatment, the Center for Substance Abuse Prevention and the Center for Mental Health Services, acknowledging the impact of violence and the role of physical and sexual abuse in the lives of women with serious mental illnesses, have responded by collaborating on the development and administration of this new study. This research is looking at women with alcohol, drug abuse and mental health disorders who have histories of violence. Knowledge that is gained from this multi-site, multi-center study is expected to be useful in advancing national, state and local policy that affects how the various service systems respond to women with co-occurring disorders who have histories of violence, and their children.

## MAILING LISTS FOR SOCIAL WORKERS

### Child Abuse Prevention Network

`http://child-abuse.com/elists.html`

Mailing lists for professionals in child abuse prevention and treatment.

### cti-soc-work-uk

`http://www.jiscmail.ac.uk/lists/cti-soc-work-uk.html`

CTI Human Services maintain this list to allow social work teachers in the UK, and international colleagues, to discuss the use of educational and learning technology in social work education. Information on new developments, publications, software, workshops, and conferences may also be posted.

### Gender-Related Electronic Forums

`http://www-unix.umbc.edu/~korenman/wmst/forums.html`

Gender-Related Electronic Forums is an annotated, frequently updated, award winning listing of publicly accessible electronic forums related to women or to gender issues.

### Internet Discussion Lists for Social Workers

`http://www.rit.edu/~694www/bpd/lists.htm`

Dozens of email lists from the BPD site at Rochester Institute of Technology.

### Mental Health Mailing Lists

`http://mentalhealth.miningco.com/library/weekly/aa060297.htm`

Mailing lists from the Mining Company.

### Psychology and Support Mailing List Pointer

`http://www.grohol.com/mail.htm`

Alphabetic listing of dozens of support-oriented and professional mailings lists.

### Social Work Access Network

`http://www.sc.edu/swan/listserv.html`

One of the most comprehensive listings of social work relevant discussion groups is the Social Work Listservs page maintained by the SWAN. The list references nearly 60 mailing lists related to a variety of aspects of social work practice.

### Social Work Resources

`http://www.clinicalsocialwork.com/socialwork.html#MAILING`

Lists of mailing lists from Pat McClendon, a social work from Louisville, Kentucky.

### Web Resources for Social Workers

`http://www.cahs.colostate.edu/sw/lists.html`

An extensive list of listservs from the site at Colorado State.

*Research Navigator Guide: Helping Professions*

# Other Online Resources

### Social Work Supersite

`http://www.ablongman.com/sw`

This new resource targets the eight zones of social work: Introduction to Social Work, Social Work Practice, Social Welfare Policy, Child Welfare, Research and Statistics, Field Practicum/Internship, Family Therapy, and Human Behavior in the Social Environment (including Lifespan Development). Each zone includes web links, practice tests, policy updates, election updates, accreditation standards, and more.

### Allyn & Bacon Mentoring Site

`http://www.ablongman.com/mentor`

This innovative and exciting program has been designed to help you get the most out of your social work experience by interacting with mentors in key areas of practice and policy.

For each practice/policy area, there is a mentor who is available to answer your questions and provide valuable feedback on his or her

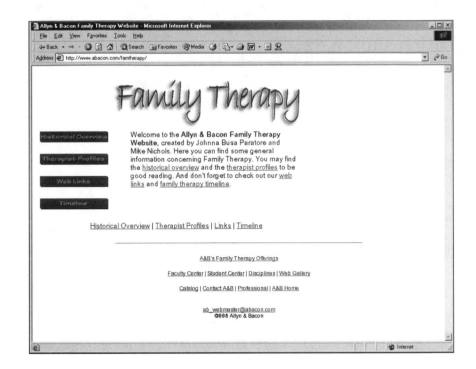

specific area of practice. The mentor will answer questions once a week. In addition, at the beginning of each month, the mentor will present a case that he or she has worked on in the past, or is currently working on. The case will challenge program participants to think critically about the situation at hand, consider what theories would be most effective, and decide what specific practice skills would work best.

### Allyn & Bacon Family Therapy Site

`http://www.ablongman.com/famtherapy`

Created by Johanna Busa Paratore and Mike Nichols, this site provides general information concerning Family Therapy, featuring a historical overview, therapist profiles, web links, and a family therapy timeline.

### Companion Web Sites

`http://www.abinteractive.com/gallery`

Our Companion Web sites use the Internet to provide you with various opportunities for further study and exploration. The CW offers study content related to the text, as well as multiple choice, true/false, and essay questions that can be forwarded to your instructor or graded instantly. For a full list of texts that offer Companion Web sites, please visit the Web site Gallery at **www.abinteractive.com/gallery.**

*Research Navigator Guide: Helping Professions*

# Glossary

## Your Own Private Glossary

The Glossary in this book contains reference terms you'll find useful as you get started on the Internet. After a while, however, you'll find yourself running across abbreviations, acronyms, and buzzwords whose definitions will make more sense to you once you're no longer a novice (or "newbie"). That's the time to build a glossary of your own. For now, the Webopedia gives you a place to start.

**alias**  A simple email address that can be used in place of a more complex one.

**AVI**  Audio Video Interleave. A video compression standard developed for use with Microsoft Windows. Video clips on the World Wide Web are usually available in both AVI and QuickTime formats.

**bandwidth**  Internet parlance for capacity to carry or transfer information such as email and Web pages.

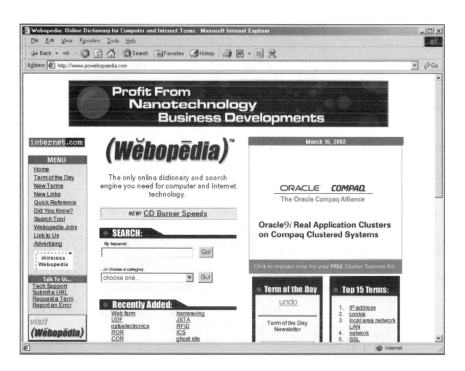

**browser** The computer program that lets you view the contents of Web sites.

**client** A program that runs on your personal computer and supplies you with Internet services, such as getting your mail.

**cyberspace** The whole universe of information that is available from computer networks. The term was coined by science fiction writer William Gibson in his novel *Neuromancer,* published in 1984.

**DNS** See *domain name server.*

**domain** A group of computers administered as a single unit, typically belonging to a single organization such as a university or corporation.

**domain name** A name that identifies one or more computers belonging to a single domain. For example, "apple.com".

**domain name server** A computer that converts domain names into the numeric addresses used on the Internet.

**download** Copying a file from another computer to your computer over the Internet.

**email** Electronic mail.

**emoticon** A guide to the writer's feelings, represented by typed characters, such as the Smiley :-). Helps readers understand the emotions underlying a written message.

**FAQs** Frequently Asked Questions

**flame** A rude or derogatory message directed as a personal attack against an individual or group.

**flame war** An exchange of flames (see above).

**ftp** File Transfer Protocol, a method of moving files from one computer to another over the Internet.

**home page** A page on the World Wide Web that acts as a starting point for information about a person or organization.

**hypertext** Text that contains embedded *links* to other pages of text. Hypertext enables the reader to navigate between pages of related information by following links in the text.

**LAN** Local Area Network. A computer network that is located in a concentrated area, such as offices within a building.

**link** A reference to a location on the Web that is embedded in the text of the Web page. Links are usually highlighted with a different color or underlined to make them easily visible.

**listserv** Strictly speaking, a computer program that administers electronic mailing lists, but also used to denote such lists or discussion groups, as in "the writer's listserv."

**lurker** A passive reader of an Internet *newsgroup* or *listserv.* A lurker reads messages, but does not participate in the discussion by posting or responding to messages.

**mailing list** A subject-specific automated email system. Users subscribe and receive email from other users about the subject of the list.

**modem** A device for connecting two computers over a telephone line.

**newbie** A new user of the Internet.

**newsgroup** A discussion forum in which all participants can read all messages and public replies between the participants.

**plug-in** A third-party software program that will lend a Web browser (Netscape, Internet Explorer, etc.) additional features.

**quoted** Text in an email message or newsgroup posting that has been set off by the use of vertical bars or > characters in the left-hand margin.

**search engine** A computer program that will locate Web sites or files based on specified criteria.

**secure** A Web page whose contents are encrypted when sending or receiving information.

**server** A computer program that moves information on request, such as a Web server that sends pages to your browser.

**Smiley** See *emoticon.*

**snail mail** Mail sent the old fashioned way: Write a letter, put it in an envelope, stick on a stamp, and drop it in the mailbox.

**spam** Spam is to the Internet as unsolicited junk mail is to the postal system.

**URL** Uniform Resource Locator: The notation for specifying addresses on the World Wide Web (e.g. http://www.abacon.com or ftp:// ftp.abacon.com).

**Usenet** The section of the Internet devoted to *newsgroups.*

**Web browser** A program used to navigate and access information on the World Wide Web. Web browsers convert html coding into a display of pictures, sound, and words.

**Web page** All the text, graphics, pictures, and so forth, denoted by a single URL beginning with the identifier "http://".

**Web site** A collection of World Wide Web pages, usually consisting of a home page and several other linked pages.